El Palacio Real:

Fortress and Castle
built by order of the
Spanish crown 1610~1612
Seat of Government
under three flags~Spanish
Mexican & American ~
From 1610 to 1910, the
residence of over a hundred
Governors & Captains General
The oldest public building
in the United States~

NEW MEXICO'S
PALACE OF THE GOVERNORS

History of an American Treasure

EMILY ABBINK

MUSEUM OF NEW MEXICO PRESS   SANTA FE

Project director and photo research: Mary Wachs
Design and production: Deborah Flynn Post
Maps: Deborah Reade
Manufactured in Singapore
10 9 8 7 6 5 4 3 2 1

Library of Congress Cataloging-in-Publication Data

Abbink, Emily.
New Mexico's Palace of the Governors : history of an American treasure / by Emily Abbink.
    p. cm.
ISBN 978-0-89013-500-6 (paperbound : alk. paper)
1. Palace of the Governors (Santa Fe, N.M.)—History.   2. Palace of the Governors (Santa Fe, N.M.)—Pictorial works.   3. Santa Fe (N.M.)—Buildings, structures, etc.   4. Governors—Homes and haunts—New Mexico.   5. Historical museums—New Mexico—Santa Fe.   6. Governors—New Mexico—Biography.   7. Santa Fe (N.M.)—Biography.   8. Santa Fe (N.M.)—History.   9. New Mexico—History.   I. Title.
F804.S28P344 2007
978.9'56—dc22   2007004473

Museum of New Mexico Press
Post Office Box 2087
Santa Fe, New Mexico 87504

Contents

A C K N O W L E D G M E N T S

Special thanks to Frances Levine, of the Palace of the Governors, and Mary Wachs, of Museum of New Mexico Press. Without their vision and assistance this project would never have come to be. I'd also like to thank Dedie Snow, Stephen Post, Dave McNeece, Julia Clifton, Cary McStay, Daniel Kosharek, Tomas Jaehn, Louise Stiver, Nelson Foss, Debby King, Robin Gavin, Tom Chavez, the folks behind the scenes at Museum of New Mexico Press, and many others who offered encouragement and help. This book was indeed a group effort and could not have happened without them.

Finally, I'd like to thank my family for their patience and support.

Photographs pages 1, 2, 3, 5, and at left
by Sharon Stewart, 2007.

D E D I C A T I O N

Nⁿew Mexico's history is the story of families and communities resisting, adjusting, and relying on each other. As a family home and center of important community events, the Palace of the Governors is the heart of this history.

The Spanish Crown sent Spanish and Mexican families to colonize New Mexico. Early settlement rosters list many children individually and others accompanying adults. The Spanish and Mexican newcomers found many villages of long-settled Native American families farming the Rio Grande Valley. Whether Native American, Spanish, Mexican, or Anglo-American, children played an important but unrecognized role in frontier communities.

Until statehood, few children in New Mexico attended school. Considered adults by age twelve, they farmed, herded, hunted, and traded. While few Spanish governors brought their own families to the Palace, many Mexican, Indian, and Spanish children lived and worked there as servants, stable hands, adobe makers, and soldiers. They suffered epidemics, starvation, revolts, and kidnapping. They celebrated birthdays, feast days, harvests, and hunts; played games; and cherished handmade toys. While records of Palace children are scant, the Palace would not have existed without them. This book is dedicated to them.

$\mathcal{P}REFACE$

The Palace of the Governors as seen looking northeast from the plaza. Photographed in 1977 by Art Taylor, courtesy Palace of the Governors (MNM/DCA) neg. 70213.

The Palace of the Governors is one of America's oldest public buildings of European origin. It is all that remains of Spain's *casas reales,* or royal houses, built around Santa Fe's plaza in 1609–10. The Palace's fourth hundredth anniversary marks its four centuries of serving New Mexico's people and celebrates part of New Mexico's long and exciting past.

The governor's Palace—the long, low adobe on the plaza's north side—was the seat of government. It was the oldest continuously occupied capitol in North America, housing governors from Spain, Mexico, and territorial New Mexico. Pueblo Indian rebels and Confederate troops also headquartered there. The Palace became a museum in 1909 and a designated National Historic Landmark in 1960. It is, as well, the oldest continuously used public building in the United States.

The Palace is central to New Mexico's unique heritage—a historical stage for a colorful cast of characters. Over four centuries, it has changed from a frontier capitol into an international tourist attraction and museum. Despite changing governments and uses, the Palace continues to serve as a monument and museum belonging to all New Mexicans.

Gerald Cassidy's 1921 mural of Coronado expeditionary party, installed at the U.S. Post Office in downtown Santa Fe.

1509–1609

A CENTURY of EXPLORATION

One hundred years before the Palace existed, the world was a different place. While Spaniards had found their way to Central America by 1509, none knew of New Mexico, much less wanted to build a palace there. Meanwhile, people living in the Rio Grande Valley likely heard faint rumors of strangers invading lands far to the south but never dreamed they would come their way.

The following century, from 1509 to 1609, would forever change the lives of Europeans and Native Americans. Excited by the discovery of rich inland empires in the Americas, Spain explored the mainland and coasts, searching for treasure and a water passage to Asia. These projects set off a chain of events that eventually led to the building of Santa Fe's Palace in 1609/1610.

SPANISH EXPLORERS

The splendor of the Far East had captivated Europeans ever since Marco Polo's fabulous thirteenth-century travel reports. Overland trade routes gave Europeans

1510.... **VASCO NÚÑEZ DE BALBOA** establishes Santa Maria de la Antigua del Darién (in modern-day Panama), the first European mainland settlement approximately one hundred years before the founding of Santa Fe

1513.... **VASCO NÚÑEZ DE BALBOA** marches across Panama and finds the Pacific Ocean

1513.... **JUAN PONCE DE LEÓN** explores Florida

1519.... **HERNÁN CORTÉZ** conquers the Aztecs

1528.... **ALVAR NÚÑEZ CABEZA DE VACA** is shipwrecked off the Florida coast

1565.... **THE SPANISH ESTABLISH** Saint Augustine, Florida

1587.... **THE ENGLISH ESTABLISH** a colony on Roanoke Island (abandoned)

1607.... **THE ENGLISH ESTABLISH** the Jamestown Colony in Virginia. Jamestown is abandoned after 1699

*Pre-Spanish, Tewa-area pottery: Santa Fe
Black-on-white (AN43863) and Bandelier
Black-on-cream (AN47026). Courtesy Museum of
Indian Arts and Culture/Laboratory of
Anthropology (MNM/DCA).*

access to Asian silks, spices, and gold but were slow, expensive, and dangerous. In the Middle East and Central Asia, middlemen controlled trade with high taxes. Europeans wanted to find a sea route to China.

Spain and Portugal became major maritime powers, racing to discover a sea route east. Not only would ships carry more goods faster, but claiming Asian ports would ensure European rights to rich eastern trade. Portugal jumped ahead, sailing south around Africa to India in 1498. Portuguese forts and trading posts soon controlled this sea route.

Spain's King Ferdinand and Queen Isabella took a chance on a proposal to reach China by sailing west. They knew that if scholars were right—that the world was round—then Asia had to be west of the horizon by just a few weeks. The monarchs provided funding, and Christopher Columbus set out in October 1492. Instead of China, he encountered the Americas.

Within decades, the Spanish had reached the Pacific and conquered the dazzling Aztec and Inca empires. Rumors of gold fueled Spain's desire for wealth. Conquistadors pushed into northern Mexico, locating rich silver mines and pearl fisheries. Spanish ships explored the Gulf Coast, hoping the Mississippi River might link the Atlantic and Pacific oceans.

At the same time, the Spanish passionately believed that their Catholic faith was the only true religion. Loyalty to Spain and the church were one in the same. Spain's pledge to spread this loyalty consumed the conquistadors.

NATIVE NEW MEXICANS

Around A.D. 1300, many Pueblo peoples lived along the Santa Fe River in adobe and masonry villages arranged around plazas. Villagers farmed irrigated fields of corn, beans, and squash near where the Palace would be built centuries later. They made Black-on-white pottery, hunted for deer and elk, and traded.

*Tyuoni Pueblo ruins at Bandelier National Monument, ca. 1910, abandoned before Spanish
exploration. Photo by Jesse Nusbaum, courtesy Palace of the Governors (MNM/DCA) neg. 28693.*

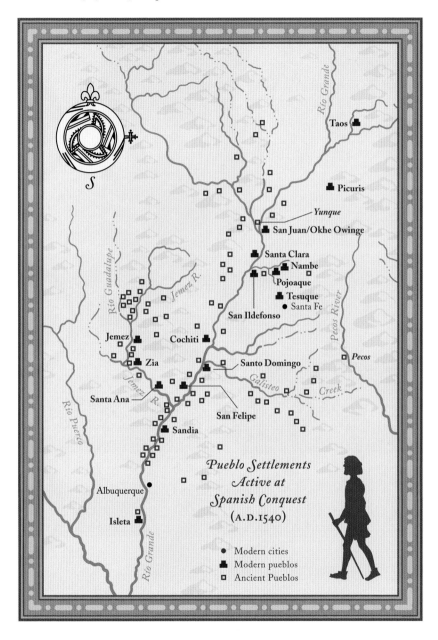

Pueblo settlements ca. AD 1540. Map by Deborah Reade.

Ancient trails fanned out in all directions, connecting people, goods, and ideas from Mexico, the Pacific, and the Great Plains.

Pueblo farmers abandoned their valley villages well before 1509, withdrawing to a few larger towns. The first Spanish explorers arriving in New Mexico during the mid-1500s encountered many villages but none along the Santa Fe River.

THE PALACE'S STORY BEGINS

In 1536 four exhausted castaways staggered into northern Mexico with a fantastic tale. They were the only survivors of a shipwrecked Spanish expedition that had been exploring Florida's coast in 1528. Their leader, Alvar Núñez Cabeza de Vaca, had pulled his crew through eight years of captivity, starvation, and desert wandering. The four survivors, including the Moorish slave Esteban, had escaped their coastal captors, becoming traders among Texas Indian tribes. Slowly they had made their desperate way south and west, following the Rio Grande, selling trinkets, and curing the sick. Friendly southern New Mexico farmers had helped them along. Trading and healing, the ragged band turned south, finding Spanish settlers at last. Cabeza de Vaca and his men were the first Europeans to see the North American interior.

While far south of the Palace's future home, the castaways' trek nonetheless started the whole New Mexico venture. Within seventy-five years, both Santa Fe and the Palace would be in place. Their terrifying adventures astonished the northern Mexico colonists. The Spanish, desiring more treasure, heard what they wanted to hear. Might Cabeza de Vaca's northern villages be another fabulous civilization? Might they be the legendary "lost cities of gold"? Did the large river (the Rio Grande) connect to the Pacific Ocean? Would the dry, rugged land-scape—like northern Mexico—yield silver mines? Wasn't it Spain's duty to bring the Catholic faith to those who had helped these heroic survivors?

Alvar Nuñez Cabeza de Vaca crossing the Great American Desert. From an engraving published in Harper's New Monthly Magazine, *July 1880. Courtesy Palace of the Governors (MNM/DCA) neg. 71390.*

On the mud roofs of Zuñi. N.M.

Zuni Pueblo, ca. 1890, photographed by Ben Wittick. Courtesy Palace of the Governors (MNM/DCA) neg. 16440.

Excavated Kuaua Pueblo, where Coronado forced Tiwa villagers to shelter his men, 1540–41. Courtesy Palace of the Governors (MNM/DCA) neg. 191708.

In 1539 Friar Marcos de Niza, guided by Esteban, led a small expedition north to answer these questions. Scouting ahead to mark the way, Esteban arrived at Zuni territory, where he angered or frightened the villagers into killing him. It's unclear whether Niza actually saw Zuni's adobe villages. Nevertheless, he returned to Mexico with a positive report.

Spain quickly funded a much larger expedition. Under Francisco Vásquez de Coronado, missionaries, troops, Indian translators, and wagon drivers—many in their teens or younger—headed north to Zuni in 1540. Sure of finding another Aztec Empire, Spain awaited the good news.

Coronado soon confirmed that the Zuni villages were not made of gold. Offended by Spanish arrogance, the Zuni angrily sent the stunned explorers packing. Other Indians promised larger, wealthier towns to the east. Wanting to believe, Coronado marched toward the Rio Grande.

Francisco Vásquez de Coronado. Drawing by José Cisneros, 1993, courtesy the artist.

Juan de Oñate, drawing by José Cisneros, courtesy of the artist.

Coronado forced the Kwa'wa villagers, near present-day Bernalillo, to shelter his men for the winter. He then pushed north to Taos and the Kansas plains searching for lost golden cities. Possibly Coronado heard tales of powerful Mississippi River towns, such as Cahokia, with elaborate temple mounds and pyramids.

Devastated not to find cities of gold, Coronado's men returned to Mexico in 1542. Their bitterness was well matched by the resentment they left behind. Despite Coronado's disappointing news, Spain was encouraged by reports of possible mines and farming peoples "wanting" conversion. Smaller campaigns further explored the middle Rio Grande Valley, leaving missionaries and seeds behind.

However, not until Juan de Oñate's 1598 colonizing expedition does the Palace's story really begin. While Oñate established neither Santa Fe nor the Palace, he did settle New Mexico's first colonial capital, San Gabriel, near San Juan Pueblo, several years before Santa Fe was established. In 1598 Oñate and his eight-year-old son, Crístobal, left Mexico, heading a party of four hundred men, thirty families, eighty-three wagons, mining equipment, and herds of livestock. Young Crístobal wore his own armor and weapons.

Aided by Indian scouts and translators, Oñate avoided the villages Coronado had angered fifty years earlier. Bypassing the soon-to-be Santa Fe area, Oñate marched to the Tewa pueblo, Okhe, where the Chama River joins the Rio Grande. Oñate's colonists moved into and modified abandoned pueblo rooms at Okhe, and changed the pueblo's name to San Juan. The Tewa people of Okhe/San Juan endured or tolerated these uninvited guests, at first.

Routes of the Conquistadores. Map by Deborah Reade.

DOÑA EUFEMIA

After soldiers left for Acoma, rumors of attacking Indians terrorized the settlers in Okhe/San Juan. Doña Eufemia, wife of Royal Ensign Francisco de Sosa Peñalosa, rallied the settlers, stationing twenty-four women on roofs to assist the few remaining men. Doña Eufemia was described as "a lady of distinguished beauty and singular courage and wisdom" (Cook 1993, 152–53). Gaspar Pérez de Villagrá immortalized her rooftop bravery in his epic poem *La Historia de la Nueva Mexico*.

NEW MEXICO'S FIRST POET

Gaspar Pérez de Villagrá documented the colony's earliest years in his epic poem *La Historia de la Nueva Mexico*. Villagrá accompanied Oñate, helped establish San Gabriel, and recorded the tragic Battle of Acoma. Villagrá left New Mexico in 1601 with a message for the viceroy but never returned. His epic is among the first accounts of European New World experiences. Written in verse, *La Historia* was published in Spain in 1610, fourteen years before Captain John Smith's history of Virginia. A copy rests in the Fray Angélico Chávez Library of the Palace of the Governors.

San Gabriel de Yungue excavation. Courtesy Maxwell Museum of Anthropology, University of New Mexico.

Instructed to establish a new colony, Oñate ignored royal guidelines forbidding towns near Native settlements. Perhaps Oñate felt this first encampment was only temporary. As expected, his colonists soon wore out their welcome depending on their Tewa hosts for food and shelter.

Inspired by Coronado's dreams, Oñate left, searching for silver mines, golden streets, and waterways to the Pacific. He also wanted Pueblo loyalty to Spain. When Spanish troops provoked a deadly riot at Acoma, Oñate brutally punished the villagers. Most Acomas not slaughtered or mutilated were enslaved in northern Mexico silver mines.

By 1600 Oñate had moved his colonists across the river from Okhe/San Juan to the abandoned Yungue Pueblo. He renamed it San Gabriel de Yungue. San Gabriel was New Mexico's first European capital. Colonists started a church and patched up sagging walls but established no plaza or royal palace.

In late 1600, more families and supplies arrived. All remained dependent on Tewa generosity. The settlers did no farm work. Their livestock trampled fields and attracted Apache raiders. The move to San Gabriel scarcely improved relations with Natives. By the summer of 1601, at least four hundred colonists had packed up and left. Desertion was illegal, but the group was too big to stop. When Oñate returned from exploring, he found his colony all but abandoned.

As the years dragged on, Oñate continued his romantic quests, and the colony fell apart. Spanish–Tewa relations grew more hostile. In 1607 the struggling colonists asked for Oñate's replacement. Life had hardly improved, there was no gold, and Oñate was too harsh. Although Oñate's soldiers would have preferred his son Cristobal, by then a teenager, to lead them, Mexico appointed Juan Martínez de Montoya as governor and recalled Oñate to stand trial.

Disgusted with their situation, civilian colonists requested permission to establish a new settlement. Around this time, several San Gabriel families began herding sheep along the Santa Fe River, thirty miles south. They built temporary shelters, livestock sheds, and corrals and called the camp "Santa Fe." In 1608 Montoya reported they had established a "plaza de Santa Fe" (Ivey 2003).

In 1609, eleven years after Oñate's expedition, Pedro de Peralta became New Mexico's second official governor, with orders to found a new capital.

SANTA FE'S NAMESAKE

Santa Fe, New Mexico, was named after Queen Isabella's armed city, Santa Fe de Granada, built outside the Moors' last Spanish stronghold of Granada. After Isabella finally drove the Moors from Spain in 1492, Santa Fe became a symbol of faith and Spanish royal power. Later that year in Santa Fe, Columbus received his orders to set sail. Isabella's fortified southern town became the model for New World cities, with a central plaza, royal houses, and a grid of streets.

LAWS OF THE INDIES

Unlike Oñate, Governor Peralta established his new town according to royal guidelines, at least in part. The Laws of the Indies (1573) provided a standard plan for Spanish colonial settlements, modeled after Roman and Mediterranean towns. The laws called for a central, rectangular plaza with streets leading from the four corners and midpoints. Surrounding royal buildings were to include a governor's palace, presidio (fortress), town hall, public granary, and church. The fortified plaza would provide space for military drills, markets, religious processions, and refuge during attacks.

HENRY HUDSON

As the Spanish were colonizing New Mexico, far to the northeast England's Henry Hudson searched for the Northwest Passage (between the Atlantic and Pacific oceans) with his young son, John. Sailing on behalf of Holland in the early 1600s, they braved arctic ice, stormy seas, and hostile Natives but found no connecting waterway. Like Oñate, Hudson's blind obsession endangered lives. But while Oñate suffered prison and debt for his misdeeds, Hudson paid with his life and his son's. On his last voyage, his starving, rebellious crew set them adrift amid the ice floes of Hudson Bay. Hudson's name lives on in history and place-names, but father and son were never seen again.

Arriving in November, with troops, servants, and their families, Peralta transferred headquarters and remaining settlers from San Gabriel to Santa Fe.

Peralta began building the *casas reales* in the winter in 1609, probably by enlarging existing Santa Fe sheep camp buildings and recycling materials from nearby pueblo ruins. Possibly some of the existing 1608 camp structures formed part of the original Palace core. Peralta likely did little more than lay out strings and rocks, marking Palace foundations, before the snows fell that winter. With Tesuque laborers, Palace construction was under way by spring 1610.

Santa Fe's location was better than San Gabriel's in every way. It was closer to more Native villages but not too close. Between the river and surrounding springs there was plenty of water. Nearby mountains provided fuel, construction materials, game, better defenses, and possible mineral wealth. The valley formed a natural basin where trails met the Rio Grande from all directions. Remote and landlocked, Santa Fe would depend heavily on this system of trails. The town became the capital of a huge territory, including modern New Mexico, Arizona, southern Colorado, and southern Utah.

"La Ciudad de Santa Fe." Engraving by Richard Kern for "Report of Lt. J. W. Abert of his Examination of New Mexico in the Years 1846-1847."

Spanish colonial spur from early 1600s, excavated at Pecos Pueblo. Collection of the Museum of International Folk Art, courtesy Palace of the Governors (MNM/DCA) neg. 152910.

1609–1709

A Century of Exploitation

Palace construction likely took several years. Early sections were probably built of jacal, that is, with upright, mud-plastered timbers set in trenches. Over the next decades, workers added more substantial adobe bricks. It's unknown if Governor Peralta, his servants, or their families ever actually lived in the Palace. However, the building was partly up and in use by 1620 when Friar Alonzo de Benavides arrived from Mexico City to inspect.

As foundations and walls took shape, the Palace came to symbolize Spain's power on the remote frontier. According to plans, Peralta's royal buildings enclosed a large public plaza—the heart of the town—where business of every kind took place. The plaza was much larger than it is today, extending farther east and south, possibly to the Santa Fe River.

Facing Mexico City, the Palace was the northern frontier's military headquarters. On the plaza's west side was the royal presidio (fortress), including barracks, a guardhouse, and, later, a high, protective wall with towers. The presidio

1609–10.. **Pedro de Peralta** starts building the Palace

1611...... **William Shakespeare** writes *The Tempest*

1620..... **Pilgrims settle** at Plymouth Rock

1629..... **Puritans settle** near Boston

1680..... **The Pueblo revolt** against the Spanish Colonists

1690s.... **Witch trials** take place in Salem, Massachusetts

1693–94.. **The Spanish reconquer** New Mexico

1706..... **Albuquerque** is founded

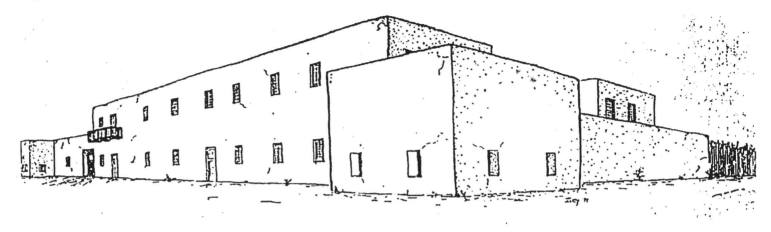

The two-story Palace of the Governors, looking northwest, may have looked like this between 1610 and 1680. Drawing by James Ivey, courtesy National Park Service.

eventually had a chapel, jail, supply rooms, wagon yards, stables, kitchens, a forge, a tannery, and slave and servant rooms.

A large fortified entrance across from the Palace opened the plaza's south side onto the Camino Real, or Royal Highway. Guarded gates at the plaza's corners and sides opened to other trails. Trenches diverted water into the plaza from the Santa Fe River to the south.

As the governor's private home, the Palace was built to enhance his status as the King's representative. The Palace had living rooms, slave and servant quarters, kitchens, and banquet halls. To the north were enclosed gardens, stables, and patios. Two stories tall, the Palace was also longer than it is today. As the colonial capitol, it included meeting rooms, archives, and storage rooms. Windows and doors opened onto an interior walled plaza and enclosed courtyards. While no early records or drawings remain, it seems the early Palace was an impressive structure.

Peralta designed the Palace to exhibit his power and cultural superiority to both settlers and Natives. Palace furnishings were lavish, meant to create desire for an aristocratic lifestyle. Candlesticks, chess pieces, Chinese porcelain, canopy beds, and chocolate sets expressed Spanish ideals. Appreciation for the value of such items encouraged loyalty to King and Church and proved their owners were successful and powerful in the Spanish system. Also to symbolize Spanish prestige, the Palace had a formal dining room for entertaining important visitors, a ballroom, and a library of history and law books. At least two Palace rooms had patterned adobe brick floors. The early Palace represented Spain's values and worldview.

Tewa polychrome bowl, 1600–30, discovered in the 1965 Palace excavations.

Seventeenth-century adobe block floor, Palace excavation of 1965. Courtesy Museum of Indian Arts and Culture/Laboratory of Anthropology (LA4451).

Eighteenth-century set for making hot chocolate. Photo by Blair Clark, courtesy Palace of the Governors.

By the mid-1600s, the Palace had at least eighteen rooms of differing sizes and purposes. In 1641 the Palace hosted a triple wedding ceremony, joining three members of the Godoy family with three members of the Romero–Robledo family. No doubt young guests, as well as servants, were present. Already the Palace served as a center for social as well as political and economic activities in New Mexico.

HOW PEOPLE SAW THE PALACE

The Palace stored items hauled to New Mexico in Mexican supply wagons. From Palace storerooms, rich colonists bought wine, chocolate, sugar, house furnishings, fine clothing, and maiolica pottery. Laborers received necessary shoes, cloth, blankets, and metal tools.

For wealthy settlers, the Palace represented fortunes to be made, glory to be found, and pride in Spain as a world power. The Palace symbolized continuity as governors came and went. It was a link with all that was considered familiar

Pre-revolt maiolica bowl or plate fragments from 2003 Palace excavations. Photo by Blair Clark, courtesy Office of Archaeological Studies, Museum of New Mexico.

Tewa Red Ware soup bowl and plate from the seventeenth century, probably made by Pueblo Indians living south of Santa Fe. Excavated 2003–04 at the Palace of the Governors. Photos by Carol Price, courtesy Office of Archaeological Studies, Museum of New Mexico.

Sankawi Black-on-cream narrow-rim soup bowl, AD 1500–1700, excavated 2003–04 at the Palace of the Governors. Photo by Carol Price, courtesy Office of Archaeological Studies, Museum of New Mexico.

Ancient ruins of Pueblo Bonito, Chaco Canyon, once a center of far-reaching political power.

Photo by Harold D. Walter, courtesy Palace of the Governors (MNM/DCA) neg. 128725.

and "civilized." Poorer settlers looked to the Palace for protection, direction, and equipment. It was the hub of their world.

Missionaries shared some of these views, but they also believed the Palace undermined their authority. Palace and church policies often conflicted. According to missionaries, the Palace encouraged conflict by competing for Indian labor, encouraging outlawed native dances, and monopolizing supplies, trade, and taxes.

What local Indians may have thought of the Palace at first is unknown. Some came there to trade or receive supplies. Others came for paid work, to report problems, or to serve a Palace jail sentence or forced labor. Still others watched from afar for raiding opportunities. For many, the Palace certainly represented lack of freedom, if not suffering and abuse.

However, at least the Palace was stationary and avoidable for Indians. Missions, on the other hand, were located in every village, placing Indians under daily scrutiny. Whether Pueblo legends painted strong central power as good or bad remains unknown; some Pueblos likely remembered stories of the once–mighty ancestral villages such as Pueblo Bonito at Chaco Canyon. That the Pueblo admired the Palace's power is evident, as later they captured it and governed from its walls. At best, New Mexico's Native populations viewed the Palace with mixed emotions.

PALACE LIFE

Early Palace governors were selected from wealthy Spanish families as a reward for their military or civil service. Such men were usually older; their children often grown. Since appointments were temporary, few governors brought their families to suffer frontier hardships. Younger children usually stayed in Mexico or Spain for school.

MISSION

Spain was as committed to spreading the Catholic faith as to establishing new colonies. The Church sent friars to live in the pueblo towns to teach religion and Spanish culture. These missionaries soon directed the villagers to build churches and living quarters and produce woven blankets, hides, and grain for mission use or sale in Mexico. They also required the Pueblo people to embrace Catholicism and shun their own traditional beliefs. Few Native New Mexicans cared for this arrangement. Unlike the Palace officials in Santa Fe, however, the missionaries lived in their midst and were difficult to ignore or avoid.

Double-barred brass cross recovered from 1974–75 Palace excavations. Courtesy Palace of the Governors (MNM/DCA) neg. 65260.

Servants and their children in a New Mexico courtyard.
Harper's, *April 1885.*

However, all governors brought servants and slaves (including children), sometimes as many as thirty. So while few "royal" children lived in the Palace, many servant children did. Young Mexican and Pueblo servants kindled fires, swept, stirred soups and peeled vegetables, and washed dishes and clothes. They drove wagons, fed horses, herded sheep, and fought as soldiers. Enslaved children built adobe walls, wove blankets, and tanned hides for sale to Mexico.

Palace children witnessed many historic events. Some poured wine at formal dinners for important visitors. Others brought candles, quills, and ink for the governor's letters. They enjoyed violins and sweets at Palace dances. They trembled when Indians attacked or missionaries argued, and they carried food to Palace prisoners.

In the plaza, deserters and rebels were hanged, military expeditions rode off, and supply trains pulled in. Children heard cannons boom in celebration of new governors and kings. They swung incense burners in church processions. Others dared watch plaza Indian dances forbidden by the church. Under the Palace portal, children traded for fruit, kicked homemade balls, and played tag.

Epidemics of smallpox, measles, and whooping cough regularly swept through New Mexico. While most devastating to Native populations, disease killed and weakened young colonists, too. Drought and starvation affected all children throughout the province.

Around the plaza, about thirty small adobe residences housed Spanish settler families. South of the Santa Fe River in the barrio de San Miguel lived many Apache, Pueblo, and Mexican Indian families. Their small homes and gardens clustered around a chapel. The Spanish hired them as weavers, blacksmiths, wagon drivers, carpenters, and builders. Many barrio women and children cooked and cleaned at the Palace.

Spanish pioneer woman ca. 1650, drawing by José Cisneros, courtesy the artist.

WITCHCRAFT

Magic potions and charms were popular among seventieth-century New Mexicans. More dangerous were spells cast in revenge or jealousy, sometimes resulting in death. One early Santa Fe woman was rumored to bewitch children with an evil eye and to fly unseen to spy on her enemies. Since witchcraft was a crime against church and state, complaints were brought to the Palace for investigation. Governors handled these accusations through legal channels, mostly avoiding the hysteria and witch hunts that occurred in Salem, Massachusetts, in the 1690s.

Feast Day of San Estévan at Acoma Pueblo. Scribner's, *December 1891.*

TENSIONS MOUNT

Missionaries expected Indian villagers to build churches and herd mission flocks. The Palace demanded they serve as scouts and soldiers and pay taxes in the form of woven goods and grain. Settlers needed their help in cleaning ditches and harvesting. Missions, government, and settlers all depended on income from Indian-produced goods sold south. Somehow, the Pueblo Indians had to support themselves as well.

Although the governor had ultimate authority, a power struggle over Indian labor soon developed, catching the Pueblo in the middle. As bitter tension grew between palace and church, each side baited the other while ignoring Pueblo needs and their fully functional and satisfactory religion and economy.

In return for exclusive trading rights, some governors allowed Native dances at the Palace. But missionaries harshly whipped Indians for dancing and resented this lack of support plus being bypassed in valuable trade relations. Missionaries also objected to Apache slaves being sold to Mexican mines for the governor's profit. Slaving, or capturing Native slaves to sell, provoked retaliatory raids on Spanish and Pueblo villages and disrupted important trade relations.

Friars accused Governor Luís de Rosas of enslaving Indian weavers. In return, Rosas expelled all Santa Fe clergy, beating two with a stick. Recalled in 1641, Rosas was mysteriously murdered before he could return to Mexico.

The situation grew worse, forcing Indians and settlers to take sides. Adding a complex layer were the growing social ties between Pueblos and settlers created by military service, trade, and marriage. Where did loyalties lie? Soon neither church nor state commanded much respect from the common people.

San Ildefonso basket dance ca. 1920. The seventeenth-century church tried to ban Pueblo dances.
Photo by Sheldon Parsons, courtesy Palace of the Governors (MNM/DCA) neg. 106877.

Governor Bernardo López de Mendizábel and his wife, Doña Teresa, arrived at the Palace in 1659 with an ornate carriage, costly bed, gilded writing desk, silver dining ware, and expensive velvet clothes and shoes. Mendizábel angered both settlers and the church by paying Pueblo laborers top wages to harvest salt and piñon nuts, weave blankets, and tan hides for his own profit, thus leaving church and settlers without herders, farmers, or builders.

It was the governor's job to distribute basic necessities and sell luxury items from Palace stores. Governors were expected to profit, but Mendizábel's huge markups caused great hardship. He enslaved Apaches for resale and invited Tesuque villagers to dance as Palace entertainment. When Mendizábel returned in chains to Mexico City, no one came to his defense.

Meanwhile, Spanish soldiers raided kivas, destroyed sacred masks, humiliated Pueblo leaders, and overtaxed villagers. Deadly smallpox and a long devastating drought brought starvation and misery. Yet missionaries forbade Pueblo rain dances.

The final straw came in 1675, when Governor Juan Francisco de Treviño arrested forty-seven Pueblo medicine men for witchcraft. Those not hanged were jailed in the Palace and publicly whipped. More than seventy warriors brandishing war clubs and leather shields barged into the Palace, demanding their release.

Terrified, Treviño backed down. Their holy men freed, the warriors had learned a valuable lesson: with planning, secrecy, and a united front, resistance was possible. One of the freed medicine men, Po'pay of Okhe Pueblo, vowed to capitalize on this lesson.

PUEBLO REVOLT: 1680–96

The major event of the Palace's first century, the Pueblo Revolt had local and worldwide consequences. The rebellion was the first successful American resistance against a colonial power, nearly one hundred years before the Revolutionary War of 1775–83. The Pueblo Revolt of 1680 inspired Native protest throughout colonial Spain for the next two hundred years.

While Native Americans viewed their struggle as a holy war, the Spanish saw it as humiliating, disloyal, and satanic. The impact on the Palace was staggering in terms of its appearance, occupants, use, and symbolic value. However, few records remain of what happened inside the Palace during the rebellion.

TROUBLE BREWING

Standing before the Palace, Governor Antonio de Otermín mopped his brow in the August sun. Repairs on the plaza's main gate were complete. Otermín sighed. What good were gates without soldiers and weapons to guard them? He scanned clusters of Indians around the plaza. Two Tesuque men staggered under loads of firewood. Newly captured Apache children fearfully awaited sale. Were the rumors true? Were the Natives planning another revolt? The Chihuahua supply train was due any week. A few gifts might quiet the grumbling. A little rain would help, too. Otermín retreated under a shaded portal. He'd worry about it later.

Iron lance point from 1974–75 Palace excavations. Courtesy Palace of the Governors (MNM/DCA) neg. 65261.

THE HATED SPANISH

Through the kiva's dim interior, Po'pay watched the last sandaled feet climb up the ladder. His runners carried *quipus*, knotted ropes, signaling that the time had come. Po'pay paced, the hearth fire casting jumpy shadows on the walls. There had to be absolute secrecy for everything to work. Po'pay scowled and spat in disgust, remembering the Palace jailer's stinging whip. The gall, to punish holy men praying for rain! How could some of his own people remain faithful to these arrogant, alien dogs? Or believe their foolish religion? Po'pay stared into the embers. It was almost time.

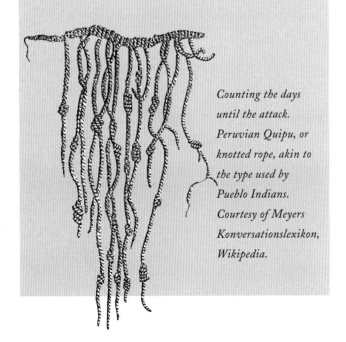

Counting the days until the attack. Peruvian Quipu, or knotted rope, akin to the type used by Pueblo Indians. Courtesy of Meyers Konversationslexikon, Wikipedia.

As luck would have it, on August 9, 1680, Governor Antonio de Otermín's men seized two young Tesuque runners, Nicolás Catua and Pedro Omtua, spreading the secret signal to revolt. Their plans discovered, the rebels acted fast. Rising up the next day, they murdered one-quarter of New Mexico's Spanish colonists, including missionaries, and kidnapped many women and children. During the next panic-filled days, more than one thousand survivors and their livestock fled to the Palace's walled plaza.

Thousands of armed and mounted Pecos, Galisteo, and San Marcos warriors, many likely in their teens, surrounded Santa Fe, taunting the Spanish to surrender. Governor Otermín refused. More squads arrived from Taos, Picuris, Jemez, and Keresan villages, plus Apache and Navajo allies. Po'pay and his opposition forces had assembled more than eight thousand troops against fewer than two hundred arms-bearing colonists.

On August 12, 1680, the rebels attacked, shooting arrows, burning roofs, and battering the plaza's fortified walls. With mounting horror, the trapped refugees, including many children, tended the wounded and loaded guns amid the frightful din and smoke.

The bloody siege lasted nine days. Otermín led two desperate forays outside the plaza gates, but more warriors laid siege. Shot in the chest and face, Otermín rallied the settlers to defend their Palace refuge.

Inside the royal compound, provisions ran low. Animals died; people would be next. How far had the revolt spread? Were there other survivors? Was help coming? Where were the supply wagons from Mexico?

Then the Pueblo forces cut off the water supply.

Pueblo runners alerted allied villages to rise up against the Spanish.
Harper's, *May 1885.*

DOCUMENTED EVIDENCE OF
SANTA FE–AREA KIDS

Cristóbal de Anaya was born near Santa Fe in the late 1620s. He was baptized and confirmed by Friar Benavides during his inspection. Cristóbal started soldiering at age eleven. Decades later, in 1680, Cristóbal, his wife, and six of their children were killed in their homestead by Santo Domingo rebels. Another young son was kidnapped.

The choice was clear: leave or die. Forced to abandon the Palace, Otermín led his defeated settlers down the Camino Real to El Paso, the nearest sanctuary. While some rode horses or jolted along in carts, most walked, carrying possessions or young children. Stunned and terrified, young and old, they could scarcely believe what had happened. As stricken families cast a last glance at the smoking, battered Palace, glorious dreams of empire vanished.

From the mesa tops, mounted Native troops watched the miserable refugees depart. There was no need to capture or kill anymore—their plan had worked. The Palace was empty, and the triumphant dream of freedom had come true.

YEARS OF INDEPENDENCE

For the next twelve years, New Mexicans were free of Spain. The El Paso fugitives longed to retake the Palace but lacked soldiers and supplies. Encouraged by the Pueblo success, other northern Mexico tribes rebelled against abusive Spanish control.

What happened to the Palace, former capitol of enemy authority, during these years of independence? While no written records exist, captured Pueblo informants filled in some of the story.

New Mexicans defiantly converted the Palace into a three-to-five–story, E-shaped pueblo fortress. They built pueblo-style fireplaces and filled in doors and walls. Additional interior walls divided the pueblo/palace into smaller living rooms with large storage and fire pits. More than one thousand Tano and Tewa Pueblo people occupied the structure. Santa Fe's large enclosed plaza was divided in two, with a kiva in each side.

Just how much of the royal compound was burned or remodeled into the new pueblo/palace is unknown. While modern archaeologists have discovered little clear evidence of revolt-era construction, they have found clues supporting informant reports. Excavators have uncovered storage and fire pits, foundations, divided rooms, bone, pottery, and interior water trenches. Returning Spanish described similar details.

To further fortify their stronghold, the Pueblo built towers and a high wall surrounding the compound. A single, sturdy gate opened to the south. Just outside the walls, they planted crops, much as the settlers had done before. Did the new Native residents hope they'd retain Palace power and status? Did Po'pay plan to extend Spanish-style centralized authority over all? Had the revolt turned the rebel leaders into the very people they'd fought so hard to drive away?

From the pueblo/palace, Po'pay ordered a return to traditional Pueblo lifeways. For example, couples married in the Christian church were instructed to divorce. But Po'pay could not erase all Spanish traces. Even the "puebloized" Palace preserved Spanish architectural elements, including adobe bricks and corner fireplaces. A new culture, mixing Spanish and Pueblo, had emerged before the revolt and continued during and after. Defying Po'pay, many Christian couples stayed together. Others secretly hid forbidden Christian imagery or kept Spanish tools, weapons, foods, and livestock. The revolt split many interracial families as both Spanish and Indian members fled south.

During these independent years, droughts continued, and Apache raiding increased. Power struggles divided loyalties and weakened alliances. Luís Tupatú of Picuris replaced Po'pay as leader in 1688. Keresan, Jemez, Taos, and Pecos villages declared war on the Tano, Tewa, and Picuris, many of whom lived in the pueblo/palace. Several Pueblo groups abandoned their villages, withdrawing to defensive mesa tops. The unified purpose that had made the revolt so successful had faded.

YEARS OF INDEPENDENCE

According to Pedro Naranjo of San Felipe Pueblo, rebel leaders encouraged Pueblo people to eliminate all things Spanish from their lives and return to traditional, pre-Spanish ways. Many obliged by destroying Spanish homes, missions, church furniture, and images, and by building new pueblos along traditional plans.

OJEDA HELPS THE SPANISH

In 1689 an El Paso expedition sacked Zia Pueblo, killing most and capturing many, including Native war captain Bartolomé de Ojeda. Taken to El Paso as an interpreter and informant, Ojeda returned with Vargas in the reconquest of 1693, helping him take advantage of brewing factionalism among the Pueblo villages and those at the pueblo/palace. He also aided the Spanish in their 1693–94 campaigns.

Portrait of Don Diego de Vargas. Courtesy Palace of the Governors (MNM/DCA).

As El Paso scouting parties grew bolder and more frequent, the Pueblo knew that the Spanish would return. Obviously, the colonists would take the pueblo/palace first. In anticipation, Pueblo loyalties shifted. Some assisted Spanish scouts, calmed internal differences among Indian groups, or formed new alliances. Others fled west, fearing the bloodshed and punishing aftermath, regardless of the winner.

1693: RECONQUEST

At first, colonial fugitives in El Paso had been unable to launch a campaign to reclaim the Palace. Royal funds went to controlling northern Mexico insurgents instead. Finally, in September 1692, Don Diego de Vargas led sixty Spanish soldiers and one hundred Indian allies up the Camino Real to the pueblo/palace, center of Pueblo resistance. Vargas raised the banner that Oñate had carried north in 1598 and that Otermín had saved when he fled south in 1680.

Pueblo leader Tupatú met Vargas over cups of chocolate to swear allegiance. He accompanied Vargas to twelve other pueblos to encourage their loyalty. Vargas freed seventy-four captive settlers, including children, and appointed Juan de Ye as governor of Pecos. Missionaries baptized Native children born after 1680. This peaceful reentry had Vargas believing it was safe to bring back the exiled colonists.

Confident the Pueblo's would vacate the pueblo/palace, Vargas returned with settler families, more allies, and one hundred soldiers in December 1693. But rebels barred the gates. Forced to camp in the snow outside, Vargas tried to negotiate. After two stormy weeks, twenty-one settlers, mostly children, died from cold.

In desperation, Vargas attacked. After a bloody two-day siege, Vargas burst through the fortress walls, assisted by de Ye's Pecos troops. Soldiers poured into the plaza, fighting from room to room, finally capturing the pueblo/palace. Native warriors not killed in the battle were executed in the plaza. More than four hundred rebel women and children were enslaved.

The freezing settlers moved into the pueblo/palace and built a temporary chapel. Vargas must have lived there, too, with his many servants and advisers. Though somewhat comfortable and secure, most settlers hoped to move out and rebuild their old homes. Vargas, however, believed the pueblo/palace was safer and that restoring the presidio was more important. Vargas started building a new plaza military compound that spring.

By summer 1694, more than eleven hundred men, women, and children had moved into the pueblo/palace. Settler Agustin Saez lived with his wife and daughter above the governor's warehouse, where Vargas stored seeds, hats, shoes and clothes, chocolate pots, buckles, buttons, weapons, saddles, and tools for settlers and Indian allies. Saez climbed down from a trapdoor to steal soap and chiles but was caught and punished.

More colonial families arrived in 1695. Most lived in the pueblo/palace while planting new fields. By the late 1690s, much of the former plaza had been rebuilt. Former captive colonist Juana Domínguez and her five children, all rescued by Spanish troops, settled on the plaza's south side. Just when the double plaza reverted back to one, and whether it was as big as before, is unknown.

Vargas's reconquest was successful because of his skilled negotiations and manipulation of traditional hostilities. By capturing the pueblo/palace, the settlers gained a safe base and symbolic control. In 1694 and 1696, many New Mexican Pueblos revolted again, but no fighting occurred at the Palace.

La Conquistadora accompanied Vargas's struggle to recapture Santa Fe. Photo by Tyler Dingee, courtesy Palace of the Governors (MNM/DCA) neg. 73832.

Two Boys

In 1693 twelve-year-old Nicolás Ortiz and nine-year-old Bernardino de Sena, a Mexican orphan, accompanied Vargas north. Both boys survived the snowy siege of Santa Fe and found shelter in the pueblo/palace. Three years later, Governor Vargas rewarded Nicolás's courage in battle against Pueblo resistance. Nicolás later became captain of the Palace militia. Bernardino grew up to acquire considerable property, including the plaza that now bears his name.

Two Marías

When Pueblo rebels killed two-year-old María Naranjo's father in 1680, she and her mother were taken captive. María's uncle rescued them both twelve years later. In 1693, at age fourteen, Mexico City–born María Luisa Godines accompanied her widowed father to Santa Fe. Both Marías likely lived in the pueblo/palace during the reconquest.

Chapel of La Conquistadora, St. Francis Cathedral, Santa Fe, February 1975. Photo by Robert Brewer, courtesy Palace of the Governors (MNM/DCA) neg. 65144.

Vargas honored Pueblo loyalty with gifts of horses, firearms, clothes, trade advantages, and protection. Juan de Ye and Apache allies were allowed to host trade fairs at Pecos. The reconquest further strengthened Pueblo–Spanish family and economic ties. Soon eleven missions were reestablished at nearby Pueblo villages.

The revolt forced the Spanish to reduce taxes and slavery. Only unbaptized (non-Pueblo) Indians could be legally enslaved. The church curbed involvement in Native politics and harsh punishments for Pueblo religious practices.

Despite his successful leadership, colonists grumbled against Vargas. They blamed him for the children who froze outside the Palace, supply shortages, and the freeing of needed Pueblo slaves. Most resisted Vargas's unpopular homeland security program, which required families to stay settled in town. Others found Vargas's paid army stationed at the new presidio too powerful. After enough complaints, Vargas was recalled to Mexico City in 1697.

His successor, Governor Pedro Rodríguez Cubero, allowed private homes to be built around and away from the plaza, making the casas reales far less secure. He replaced much of the fortified Palace with six smaller, less defendable buildings. How much Cubero's new Palace followed the outlines of the original is unknown. Returning for a second term in 1703, Vargas claimed Cubero's Palace was small, poorly built, and without defense.

Vargas died on campaign in 1704. His will mentions a Palace library, including books on history, law, and religion and one cookbook. Also listed are formal clothes worn for receiving Indian leaders. The will granted freedom to Andrés, Vargas's black personal slave, after he escorted Vargas's two grown sons back to Mexico City.

Governor Francisco Cuervo y Valdés, who served from 1705 to 1707, probably left his three young sons in Mexico City for schooling. Like Vargas, he gave food, tobacco, and beads from Palace supplies to peaceful Apaches. Also like Vargas, Cuervo ordered settlers to build corrals and houses closer in for defense, but they refused. In desperation, Cuervo wrote for permission to relocate Cubero's already crumbling Palace. Permission was denied.

Governor Joseph Chacón arrived next with his wife and baby son, plus nine or ten servants. By then Cubero's "restored" Palace had so deteriorated that Chacon also wanted to demolish it. As before, the request was denied. Barely standing, the Palace turned one hundred in 1709.

SEBASTIÁN RODRÍGUEZ

Sebastián Rodríguez was Vargas's black slave and military drummer. He mustered and drilled Spanish soldiers throughout the reconquest and later campaigns. Rodríguez announced news and proclamations with a drum and bugle in front of the Palace. Born around 1642, Rodríguez came from Portuguese Guinea on Africa's northwestern coast. He lived with his wife and two sons, Melchor and Esteban, on the plaza's west side. Esteban succeeded his father as a military drummer.

Panel from the eighteenth-century Segesser hide paintings depicting historical events in late Spanish Colonial New Mexico. Photo by Blair Clark, courtesy Palace of the Governors.

1709–1809

A Century of Accommodation

The poorly rebuilt Palace marked its one hundredth year firmly back under Spanish control. Once again Spain's royal frontier headquarters, the post-revolt Palace symbolized a new Pueblo–settler alliance. New Palace policies promoted shared trade and defense, negotiations, and safe refuge from attack for all.

Throughout the 1700s, governors granted land and tools for new river valley settlements. The plaza continued as a hub, connecting trails for trade and exploration. From the Palace, Pueblo and Spanish troops mustered to track down raiding tribes.

The Palace's second one hundred years saw New Mexico's citizens grow more accommodating of one another. Sharing common interests, Natives and settlers increased trade, strengthened social ties, and defended their fields. Colonists set aside fears of Indian practices and beliefs. Pueblos willingly allied together and with settlers. As neighbors, they intermarried, solved land and

1709–10 ... THE PALACE turns one hundred

1718 ...... THE FRENCH establish New Orleans

1718 ...... THE SPANISH establish San Antonio, Texas

1769 ...... SAN DIEGO MISSION is founded in California

1775 ...... THE AMERICAN REVOLUTION BEGINS; Juan Bautista de Anza's settlers travel to California

1803 ...... THE UNITED STATES carries out the Louisiana Purchase

Puname polychrome jar ca. 1740. Santa Fe dwellers would have traded for and used such jars throughout the 1700s. Photo by Bill Acheff, courtesy El Palacio *and the Collection of Mr. and Mrs. Larry Frank.*

water issues, and pooled labor, marketing, and community assistance. Such adaptation allowed a distinctly New Mexican culture to form and endure.

According to Governor Felix Martínez, who served from 1715 to 1717, the Palace and much of the royal complex stood two stories high and included several outbuildings. However, Martínez also reported only one serviceable room with an intact ceiling in danger of collapse. It is unclear whether Governor Martínez was describing the remains of the pueblo/palace or Cubero's hasty remodeling efforts.

The new Palace complex was probably never as big or as secure as it had been before the revolt. However, Vargas's rebuilt presidio had expanded by 1715 to accommodate one hundred troops, plus slaves and servants. Probably many of these troops, slaves, and servants were boys in their teens. Martínez described the main Palace entrance opening onto a courtyard with guardhouses, a coach room, and a flour mill. Citizens worshipped in the Palace's military chapel until the main church, east of the plaza, was completed around 1717.

Most likely, the Palace was repaired and enlarged after Martínez's dismal report. A 1720 criminal case stated that Ysidro Sánchez entered the Palace through a second-floor balcony window to steal supplies from the first-floor storeroom. Sanchez stuffed stolen clothes into cracks around the Palace's outside portal. Children playing ball on the plaza soon discovered the hidden loot. In the 1720s and 1730s, governors Juan Domingo de Bustamente and Gervasio Cruzat y Góngora both mentioned improving the Palace at their own expense.

Eventually, the casas reales again included a jail, stables, a kitchen, and a garden. As in prerevolt days, the governor's Palace had private living rooms, slave and servant quarters, offices for meeting Indian and Mexican officials, a dining hall, and a ballroom.

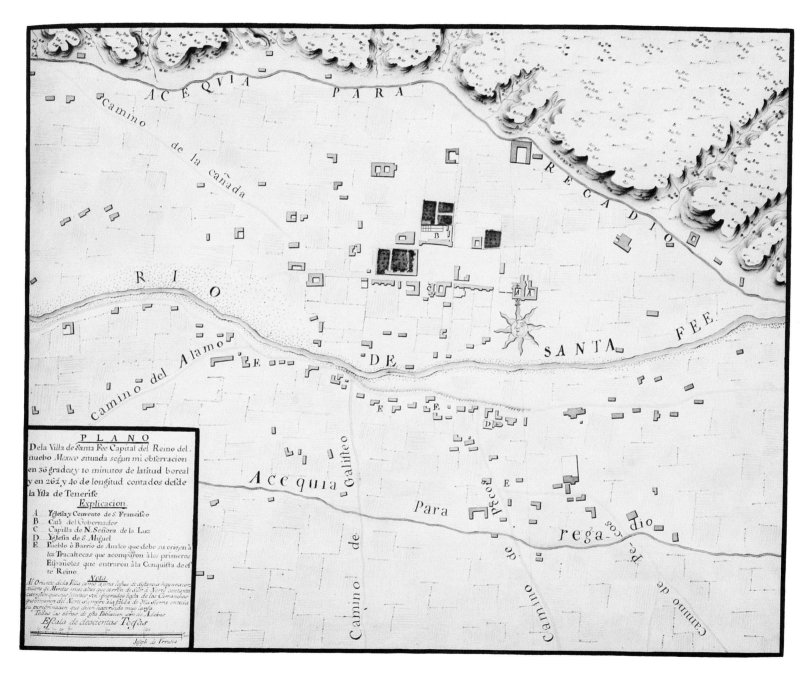

The earliest known map of Santa Fe, drawn by José de Urrutia, 1767. The original plaza of 1607
extended from the Palace east to the parish church (marked "A" on the map). Courtesy Fray
Angélico Chávez History Library and Photo Archives, Palace of the Governors (MNM/DCA).

Fiesta

In 1712, twenty years after Vargas's initial entry into the rebel plaza stronghold, Governor Chacón hosted the first Fiesta. Celebrated each September, the Fiesta commemorated September 14, 1692, when Vargas briefly and peacefully presided over the symbolic repossession of the Palace. The first Fiesta included Mass followed by a procession and pageant in the plaza, in which the Pueblo took part.

It seems likely that the royal complex did not completely surround the plaza. Although raids highlighted the need for strong defenses, it's unclear how much of the plaza's defensive walls were restored. Instead, the plaza remained open and public, with houses and stores surrounding the south side and the church to the east. As more businesses opened, the once rectangular plaza gradually shortened to a square.

During the 1700s, the plaza became a major market center for colonial commerce. Mexico sent up more supply trains, lower taxes encouraged local commerce, and trade with Plains tribes increased. New silver mines in northern Mexico demanded more New Mexican wool, blankets, piñon, salt, and slaves.

The plaza also served as military parade grounds, camping for visiting Indians, a storage yard, and a social center. Locals enjoyed religious processions, fiestas, bullfights, theater, and music there. The plaza was where criminals were hanged and thieves locked in stocks, surrounded by the items they had stolen.

At this time, Santa Fe's downtown city streets took shape, and trails from the plaza became actual roads. The Camino Real remained Santa Fe's major connection to the Río Abajo (the Lower Rio Grande south of Santa Fe), El Paso, Chihuahua, and Mexico City. The Camino Real left the plaza's south-central side, crossing the Santa Fe River, heading southeast. From the plaza's north-central side, east of the Palace, a trail ran north toward Tesuque Pueblo and beyond.

EIGHTEENTH-CENTURY LIFE

From the east, French and Anglo-Americans had crowded Plains tribes closer to Santa Fe. Comanches and Utes attacked Apache, Spanish, and Pueblo villages, stealing livestock, produce, and people. The Comanche soon controlled much of the eastern plains. New Mexicans sometimes redeemed captives at yearly Taos trade fairs and retaliated with bloody raids of their own.

Spain tried to make nomadic Indians dependent on Palace supplies. Governors invited peaceful groups for Palace feasts and gifts of food, clothes, gunpowder, and livestock. Visiting Indian leaders were given a place to stay.

Slavery was tolerated as a way to Europeanize and Christianize non-Pueblo Indians. In addition to black slaves brought from Spain, Palace and settler households often included enslaved Apache or Comanche children. On Sundays Pueblo Indians and colonists reported to the Palace for paid work. Men constructed public buildings, cleaned irrigation ditches, and cultivated gardens. Women swept, shucked corn, and baked bread.

Less obsessed by dreams of gold and glory, eighteenth-century Spain focused on protecting borders. New Mexico became a buffer between Mexico's silver mines, Plains Indians, and eastern British colonies. Drained by managing its huge colonial empire, Spain sent little aid to the isolated, northern frontier.

To boost security, the Palace and new presidio hosted many war councils. In 1714 Governor Juan Ignacio Flores Mogollón invited Pueblo leaders to plan campaigns for allied expeditions against hostile nomads. Crucial to colonial defense, Pueblo allies were given horses and guns and allowed to paint themselves, conduct religious ceremonies, and trade with enemy tribes. It was said that the governor's Palace office was decorated with enemy scalps.

VILLASUR

In 1720 a combined force of presidio soldiers and Pueblo warriors marched from the plaza under command of Lieutenant Pedro de Villasur. Ordered to check rumors of French to the north, his forces included Indian scouts and French interpreters. Near the Platte River, French and Pawnee troops launched a deadly surprise massacre against Villasur's party. Only thirteen Spanish and forty Pueblos survived the return trek to the Palace to tell the tale. Villasur was among the slain.

WITCHCRAFT

Governor Cachupín established the Abiquiu Genízaro Pueblo in 1754. It was a defensive buffer between Rio Grande farming villages and nomadic raiders from the northwest. Complaints of bewitchery and devil worship caused Cachupín to organize a trial in 1766. After much discussion, the accused witches, imprisoned at the Palace, received light sentences. No one was hanged or burned at the stake. This last major witchcraft outbreak in North America showed that New Mexico's cultural accommodation between Spanish settlers, Pueblo villagers, and nomadic tribes was well under way.

Military inspector Pedro de Rivera visited the Palace in 1726. His report resulted in improved frontier defense and protection of Pueblo warrior rights. Rivera was impressed by Pueblo bravery and loyalty, noting that women and children also fought fearlessly, defending villages with slingshots and arrows. Pueblo Indians served as military scouts, translators, and escorts. Villages became bases to launch and supply campaigns. For example, in 1732, an armed expedition to gather salt met at Galisteo Pueblo.

TRADE

While Mexico sent yearly supply trains, the supplies were not nearly enough to provide for settlers, allied Pueblos, and friendly nomads. Plaza merchants began attending trade fairs in Taos, Pecos, and Picuris. They drove pack mules to Chihuahua, Texas outposts, and, later, California missions.

But high prices drove New Mexicans to buy cheaper, illegal French goods through Plains Indian traders. French trespassers Pierre and Paul Mallet reached Santa Fe from New Orleans in 1739, quickly selling all their goods. Palace governors requested permission to legalize trade with France. The request was denied; all non-Spanish trade remained illegal.

Risking arrest, French traders, wanting Mexican silver and horses, soon established a direct trail down the Arkansas River to the plaza. Plains Indian trade also linked eastern cities indirectly with Santa Fe. This illegal foreign commerce grew, pulling the Palace, once so isolated, into world politics.

Due to Spain's troubles at home, support and contact with Santa Fe decreased. The Palace heard of Spain's new king, Ferdinand VI, in 1748, two years after his coronation. New Mexicans dutifully celebrated in the plaza, staging processions, military review, speeches, and possibly a Palace ball. But probably few New Mexicans felt much connection to the new king.

Over two terms (1749–54 and 1762–67) Governor Tomás Veles Cachupín expanded Vargas's earlier alliances to include enemy tribes. In 1751 Comanches attacked Galisteo Pueblo. With Ute and Apache allies, Cachupín set fire to surrounding woods, trapping and killing more than one hundred Comanches. By sparing the lives of captive women and children, Cachupín negotiated peace with several Comanche groups.

Meanwhile, Plains tribes noticed the Pueblo's protected and privileged status as Spanish allies. Through a policy of gifts and support, Cachupín created a multination alliance against the Comanche. Many recently hostile groups camped in front of the Palace to receive provisions and honors. Thirty years later, Governor Juan Bautista de Anza would fashion a similar alliance against the Apache.

Unfortunately for New Mexico, governors after Cachupín unraveled his hard-won negotiations. In 1760 alienated tribes raided Taos, kidnapping fifty women and children. Most never returned. Some were traced to Saint Louis and New Orleans, where they had been sold as slaves.

Governor Pedro Fermín de Mendinueta, who held office from 1767 to 1778, finished destroying Cachupín's multination treaty. Mendinueta warred with the Comanche while insulting the Navajo, Ute, Apache, and many Pueblos. By 1776 Spain had nearly lost control. Bloody pillaging ravaged New Mexico's northeastern frontier. Villagers lived in constant fear. Newly hostile tribes threatened trading, farming, and herding. Palace policies of enslaving captured Navajo, Apache, and Shoshone children further increased hostilities.

PALACE/PLAZA

Bishop Pedro Tamarón stayed in the Palace when inspecting New Mexico's missions in 1760. According to his report, Santa Fe no longer had a presidio. The fort built by Vargas and expanded in 1715 had collapsed. Despite the need for extensive military defense, soldiers were housed around town and in plaza barracks.

José de Urritia's 1767 sketch (page 49) is the earliest known Santa Fe map. It shows the plaza shrunk to its approximate modern size and shape but few Palace details. By 1766 San Francisco Street formed the plaza's south side.

Sometime in the late 1700s, the Palace lost its upper story. In 1767 the Moya brothers were caught stealing goods from the Palace warehouse by cutting through a ground-floor door. Unlike previous robbery reports, there was no mention of an upper story providing access to the merchandise.

Friar Francisco Atanasio Domínguez toured New Mexico's missions in 1776. While he reported much about church buildings and activities, the Palace completely unimpressed him. Santa Fe's "mournful appearance" offered nothing "to lift the spirits," he wrote. The plaza's south, east, and west sides had "random adobe huts, lacking both adornment and fortification." Located on the plaza's north side, the "Palace is like everything else here, and enough said" (Adams and Chavez 1956:40).

Domínguez also explored the Old Spanish Trail linking Santa Fe, through Colorado and Utah, to California's Pacific-coast missions. Unfortunately, for the Shoshone, this trail promoted easier access to captured Shoshone slaves from Nevada's Great Basin. Many French and Anglo-American trappers also used the trail illegally.

ANZA: 1778–88

Meanwhile, far to the west, Juan Bautista de Anza opened the first trail from Mexico north to California. Despite fierce weather, he successfully led 198 colonists, mostly children under twelve, to Monterey and San Francisco. Anza's expert negotiations won alliances with Colorado River tribes, allowing settlers and livestock safe passage.

Because of his frontier skills, Spain appointed Anza governor of New Mexico to reestablish Cachupín's lost peace treaties. Unfortunately, Anza's California replacements, like Cachupín's in New Mexico, shattered his peace alliances there. The Yuma Revolt of 1781 permanently closed Anza's Mexico–California route.

As Anza moved into the Palace, Comanches and Apaches ransacked northern towns. The summer before, these same tribes had killed or captured 630 villagers and stolen more than twelve hundred head of livestock. Anza's orders were to ally with the Comanche against the Apache. The Comanche warriors dressed in buffalo skins, painted their faces red, and adorned their hair with gold buttons, colored glass beads, and ribbons. The Spanish admired Comanche courage and honor, describing the Comanche as good-looking, warlike, frank, and generous.

Despite such admiration, villagers were up against Comanche chief Cuerno Verde, whom Anza called the "cruel scourge" of New Mexico (Kenner 1969:45). Cuerno Verde sported a headdress with green horns. His attendants carried a buffalo skin canopy to shade him. The Comanche chief plundered towns from Santa Fe north. Terrified villagers could scarcely tend their fields.

Portrait of Juan Bautista de Anza attributed to Fray Orei in Mexico City, 1774. Courtesy Palace of the Governors (MNM/DCA) neg. 50828.

Portion of the Urrutia's map of 1767 (see page 49) showing the Palace of the Governors, the plaza directly in front of it to the south, and La Castrense (the military chapel). Shown in outline behind the Palace of the Governors are buildings projected from cobble foundations found during the 2002–05 archaeological excavations. Solid black rectangular areas indicate orchards and gardens. Courtesy Stephen Post, Office of Archaeological Studies (MNM/DCA).

With Pueblo, Ute, and Jicarilla Apache troops, Anza ambushed and defeated Cuerno Verde in 1779, breaking Comanche resistance. In 1785 a council of Comanche chiefs elected Ecueracapa (Leather Cape) to negotiate with Anza. According to Palace eyewitnesses, Ecueracapa's "harangue of salutation and embrace of the governor after dismounting at the door of his residence exceeded 10 minutes" (Kessell 2002: 301). Anza and Ecueracapa exchanged gifts in alliance with Ute chief Moara.

The allies met at Pecos Pueblo to formalize their truce and declare war against the Apache. In exchange, the Comanche could expand west, trade at Pecos and Taos, and travel safely to the Palace for consultations. Anza also published prices to prevent New Mexican merchants from cheating their new customers.

Governor Anza appointed Ecueracapa chief of all Comanches, paid him annually in goods, and sent presidio interpreters to Comanche villages. Anza also traded Comanche captives for Spanish, Pueblo, and Apache child hostages. The Comanche returned a Spanish youth, Alejandro Martín, after eleven years of captivity. Alejandro became a government agent and Comanche interpreter.

Anza's program of gifts, councils, and trading privileges eventually secured widespread peace, much as Governor Cachupín had done. Every spring, friendly nomads camped in the plaza, waiting for Chihuahua supply wagons. Officials hoped that the nomads, once dependent on Spanish gifts, would settle down. At royal expense, the Spanish offered to educate Comanche boys in the Spanish language, customs, and faith; in 1786 Chief Ecueracapa sent his youngest son, Lahuchimpia, to be educated in Mexico City. Also in 1786, Anza distributed two hundred firearms to allied Pueblo, Ute, and Comanche chiefs to fight the Apache.

Comanche leaders, some one hundred years later, attending a peace council with Americans. Courtesy Palace of the Governors (MNM/DCA) neg. 189124.

NEW MEXICO'S EARLY ROADS

All roads led to Santa Fe's plaza. Friendly relations with the Comanche and Ute allowed the Palace to fund trail exploration, encourage trade, and protect borders. French pathfinder Pedro Vial had lived with the Comanche, serving the Palace as interpreter and Indian agent. Vial explored a route east, linking Santa Fe to San Antonio and Natchitoches. The road was "very passable in all seasons and with no risk other than the Osages, since the Comanche are already very peaceful and are our friends" (Kessell 2002: 305, 309).

Sent east in 1795 to arrange peace between the Comanche and the Pawnee, Vial met Anglo-American traders from Saint Louis. Vial figured eighteen travel days between the Palace and Saint Louis, setting the stage for the famous Santa Fe Trail twenty-five years later. Meanwhile, easier Navajo relations permitted exploration of a shorter, more direct wagon trail connecting Santa Fe and Tucson through Zuni.

Anza encouraged New Mexicans to move in closer to the plaza for security. Like others before him, he tried to relocate the casas reales, including the Palace, to a better defensive location near San Miguel Church. As before, the plans proved unpopular.

While Governor Fernando de la Concha, who served from 1788 to 1794, brought no family members, he arrived at the Palace with a household of thirty-four, including servants and their children. He wisely continued and expanded Anza's multination alliance. Drought had reduced the bison herds so much that the Comanche were without meat or hides to trade. When Chief Ecueracapa and 180 warriors came to the Palace in 1789, Concha gave them 144 bushels of corn.

Governor Concha also encouraged the "Comanchero" trade with nomadic Plains Indian encampments and far-off trade fairs. Nomadic tribes wanted bread, flour, cornmeal, cloth, and produce. In return, Comancheros, or traders, traveling with pack mules, brought back buffalo hides, furs, meat, French guns, and horses. Comancheros sometimes located missing captives, offering ransom and arranging hostage trades. Such commerce was important to New Mexico's economy. Anza's alliances continued until the early 1800s. Although Osage warriors captured eight hundred Santa Fe horses in 1790, the eighteenth century ended peacefully in New Mexico.

Anza's Elk

King Carlos III requested elk for his royal zoo. Anza's men dutifully caught eight huge animals and corralled them behind the Palace for shipment to Spain. But the elk proved nasty and expensive guests. Not only did they attack people, they ate far too much. When the elk were finally sent, at great expense, no doubt Palace residents were happy to see them go.

Anza's Nieces

While Governor Anza and his wife had no children, their Palace household included Anza's brother, his wife, and their two small daughters, Ana María and María Rosa. Governor Anza doted on his nieces. The girls were likely tutored by their aunt and mother, met powerful visiting Comanche, Ute, and Pueblo leaders, and certainly saw the elk captured for the king. In 1780–81, a smallpox epidemic killed many Pueblo and Spanish villagers. One hundred and forty-two Santa Fe residents, mostly children, died. Fortunately, Anza's nieces were spared. When his appointment ended, the sisters were teenagers. Anza's household left the Palace and moved back to Mexico.

Late eighteenth-century presidial soldier of California in official uniform, ca. 1791. Similar dress would have been seen in New Mexico's presidio at Santa Fe. Sketch by José Cordero, courtesy El Palacio.

NEW PRESIDIO: 1791

Throughout the long decades of raiding, Spain had ignored Santa Fe's repeated requests for a new presidio and more troops. The town desperately needed a central military compound to house soldiers and their families. In an emergency attack, it took more than two hours to alert soldiers scattered around town. Anza had finally convinced Spain to begin construction of a presidio in 1787. Settlers, aged fourteen to fifty, built the presidio for wages.

A presidio floor plan drawn by military engineer Juan de Pagazaurtundua shows an enclosed compound measuring one thousand by twelve hundred feet. Barracks, forming most of the perimeter, consisted of one hundred two-room apartments, plus corrals. The Palace formed the presidio compound's southeastern corner. Presidio construction created a second, enclosed plaza, north and west of the public plaza. The compound's main entrance opened to the south onto the main plaza about where Lincoln Street is today. This entrance was just west of the Palace guardhouse and jail. Later reports mention round towers at each corner of the presidio compound. The presidio enclosed an area between modern-day Washington and Grant streets and from Palace Avenue north to South Federal Place. Inside, behind the Palace, were gardens. Long portals ran along both south and north sides. The presidio was completed in 1791. More than one hundred soldiers, their families, and servants—plus a surgeon, chaplain, scouts, and Indian interpreters—moved in.

By 1800 Santa Fe was the West's largest urban center. With a population of about five thousand, it was bigger than San Antonio, Los Angeles, Monterey, or Tucson. Nearly two hundred years old, the Palace with its newly attached presidio complex remained the royal military and government seat. The official destination for important visitors and mail, the Palace also remained the colony's cultural connection with Mexico City and Spain.

Spain believed New Mexico's borders stretched from the Mississippi River to the Pacific. After the Louisiana Purchase of 1803, Spain feared that the United States would infiltrate New Mexico's eastern frontier. U.S. traders and trappers had already weakened Spain's alliances with Plains tribes to the east.

Spain's policy regarding foreigners remained clear. Most trespassers were arrested and tried in Chihuahua, although occasionally Palace governors looked the other way. Some illegals with needed skills served time in Santa Fe. For instance, in 1806 captured U.S. tailor Zalmon Coley arrived at the Palace, sentenced to sew cloaks, jackets, breeches, and vests for the garrison.

Caught by border patrols the following year, American Zebulon Pike told Governor Joaquín del Real Alencaster that he had "gotten lost" and strayed into

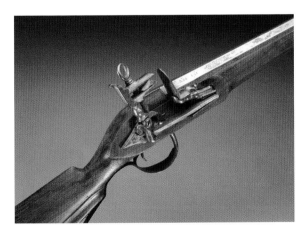

Late eighteenth-century rifle of the type used on the New Mexico frontier. Photo by Blair Clark, courtesy El Palacio and Museum of New Mexico.

Ranchitos polychrome jar ca. 1800. Photo by Blair Clark, courtesy Museum of Indian Arts and Culture/Laboratory of Anthropology (55770).

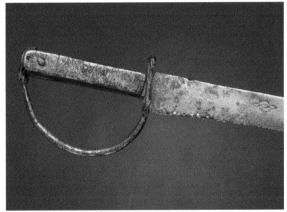

Late eighteenth-century sword used in New Mexico. Photo by Blair Clark, courtesy Palace of the Governors collection (2572).

WHITE HOUSE

In 1800, far to the east, President John Adams moved his family into the new White House in the new U.S. capital of Washington, D.C. The grand two-and-one-half-story mansion included the First Family's residence, offices, formal reception and dining rooms, and a grand ballroom. Built of white sandstone, the imposing structure was meant to symbolize the grandeur and authority of the United States. Compared to the new "presidential palace," Santa Fe's Palace seemed shabby and out-of-date.

VACCINATION

A new presidio army surgeon vaccinated hundreds of Santa Fe children against smallpox in 1804. The live vaccine was carried up the Camino Real in the arms of Mexican children inoculated for that purpose. The vaccination process, developed by English physician Edward Jenner in 1796, was eagerly accepted by Palace officials, as epidemics regularly plagued the colony.

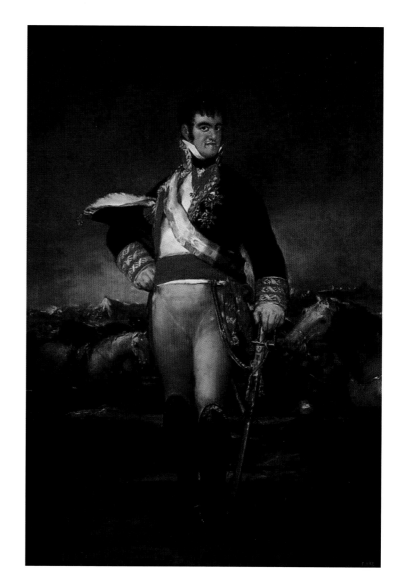

Goya's 1814 portrait of Fernando VII, King of Spain.

Spanish territory. Believing Pike to be a spy, Alencaster sent him to Chihuahua, but first treated him to a Palace dinner. According to Pike, the Palace had mud-packed floors covered with bear and buffalo skins. The meal was "rather splendid, having a variety of dishes and wines of the southern provinces, and when his Excellency was a little warmed with the influence of cheering liquor, he became very sociable" (Kessell 2002: 349).

The two chatted amiably in French, and afterward Alencaster drove Pike in his coach to see the countryside. "When we parted his adieu was 'remember Allencaster [*sic*] in peace and war,'" Pike recalled. Alencaster sent Pike to his Chihuahua trial with a new shirt and "neck cloth" (Kessell 2002: 349). Later, back in the United States, Zebulon Pike published his frontier adventures. His journal gave Americans their first glimpse of life in New Mexico. It also highlighted the lucrative market for goods waiting in Santa Fe's plaza, if only merchants could get there.

In 1808 the Spanish empire was ordered to celebrate King Ferdinand VII's coronation. Palace officials planned an elaborate four-day affair with processions, plaza bonfires, and special masses. No doubt presidio soldiers drilled and fired plaza salutes, while the Palace likely hosted a banquet and grand ball. However, Spain's new monarch would soon deny support for the colonial empire. The Palace was again crumbling as it turned two hundred, and traitorous talk of independence from Spain was in the air.

Lt. Zebulon Montgomery Pike (1779–1813). Engraving from a painting by Charles Wilson Pecke. Courtesy Palace of the Governors (MNM/DCA) neg. 7757.

El hacendado y su mayordomo *(The Hacienda Owner and His Foreman)*, *1836 hand-colored lithograph by Karl "Carlos" Nebel illustrating the fashions and horse accoutrements used in Mexico and New Mexico in the late colonial period and early nineteenth century. Courtesy Museum of Spanish Colonial Art.*

1809–1909

A Century of Political Transformation

In 1809, as the Palace turned two hundred, Spain's unstable government promoted rebellion throughout the empire. Mexico declared its independence from Spain in 1821. While Mexico suffered violence, the Palace endured no unrest. Word of Mexico's independence reached Santa Fe in September 1821. Governor Facundo Melgares announced New Mexico's new colonial status in the plaza, led a solemn procession, and pledged allegiance to Mexico.

In December Melgares received orders to honor Mexican independence with a long series of activities. Despite freezing temperatures, Melgares planned a five-day celebration. Bells rang, musicians played, and children paraded through the snow to the Palace. Richly dressed as angels, three children represented Independence, Religion, and Union. More costumed children carried flowers.

1809–10...The Palace turns two hundred

1821......Mexico declares independence from Spain

1846–48...The United States and Mexico fight the Mexican War

1848......New Mexico becomes part of the United States; the California gold rush begins

1861–65...The United States fights the Civil War

1898......The United States and Spain fight the Spanish-American War

"Mexican Lancer," from Pictorial History of Mexico and the Mexican War, *illustrated by John Frost in 1848. Courtesy Palace of the Governors (MNM/DCA) neg. 171107.*

Drilling soldiers, artillery salutes, Pueblo dancers, and Mexican flags filled the plaza. Evening festivities included public games, music, and an all-night Palace ball with lavish refreshments, open to "all persons of distinction." To his new bosses, Melgares reported that it "was an unforgettable day" (Weber 1973: 40–41). Despite such patriotism, a Mexican governor soon replaced Melgares, New Mexico's last Spanish governor.

THE MEXICAN ERA

While this political changeover in New Mexico seemed smooth, the following decades brought bloodshed. As Mexican citizens, New Mexicans briefly enjoyed many democratic freedoms, including voting rights. Comanche leader Cordero, in a blue Spanish uniform plus face paint, formally paid respect to the new Palace governor from Mexico.

However, the freedoms were short-lived. In 1836 Mexican president Antonio López de Santa Ana introduced repressive laws, raised taxes, and reduced voting rights and government support for the northern border. As Mexico cut frontier gifting, New Mexico's peace alliances dissolved. The intense raiding of the 1700s returned. Damaged by heavy rains, Anza's new presidio started slumping. New Mexican citizens were commanded to fight marauders without pay or equipment. Rebellion began to brew.

Mexico ignored the important lessons of the Pueblo Revolt and decades of frontier alliance building. Policies of respect and accommodation so carefully tended by former governors faded. New Mexico's long-dormant violent legacy against government repression soon resurfaced at the Palace door.

POOR PÉREZ

Albino Pérez became governor in 1835, just before Santa Ana's sweeping changes. New Mexicans considered Pérez an extravagant, foreign, and intellectual snob, whose purchases of gaudy clothes ran up huge debts. Pérez spent military funds on showy Palace furnishings, including gilded mirrors and costly glass windows.

Between the rain-soaked presidio and the volunteer army, colonial defense fell apart. Navajos attacked Rio Grande towns, including Santa Fe, stealing livestock and children. Lacking frontier experience, Pérez launched difficult winter campaigns in retaliation.

Grumbling villagers ambushed Pérez north of Santa Fe in 1837. After escaping back to the Palace, Pérez fled south that night but was trapped near the outskirts of town. A frenzied mob cut off his head. Mounting it on a pole, rioters raged past the Palace screaming, "Ah you robber! You will no longer extort taxes; you will no longer drink chocolate or coffee!" (Lecompte 1985, 30–34).

Camped near the plaza, revolutionaries chose José González, a buffalo hunter without political experience, as governor, but Santa Fe citizens soon jailed him in the Palace. They considered González a rebel, and deemed him neither experienced nor representative of those who wanted stable trade relations with the U.S. (González was later freed but killed in an insurgency away from Palace.) Former governor Manuel Armijo negotiated with the rebels, appointing himself governor. Calm returned to the Palace temporarily.

New Mexican mountaineer ca. 1840, drawing by José Cisneros, courtesy of the artist.

THE PALACE DURING THE MEXICAN ERA

During the Mexican period, colonists still called the governor's residence the royal Palace. Like the Spanish, Mexican governors kept the Palace fancy to impress visitors. However, nothing short of a major remodeling could disguise its poor condition. The governor's household of family and servants often moved from room to room as repairs were needed. By the 1830s, the presidio's crumbling towers had been torn down. But the decaying fort maintained sixteen-year-old Tomás Martín as official drummer to preserve appearances.

By the 1840s, the Palace's east, south, and west sides had pine portals. Public meetings and food markets took place out front and at the west end. The long, low Palace ballroom had a packed-dirt floor and door panels made of tanned hide painted to look like wood.

The Palace paid a schoolmaster to teach reading, writing, religion, and math. The first public school opened in 1826, but most wealthy families sent their children to Mexico City or Saint Louis for school. New Mexico's first printing press arrived in 1834, installed in the Palace ten years later for government printing.

COMMERCE

Since the late 1700s, foreigners from the east had trapped illegally in New Mexico. After independence, Mexico legalized foreign trapping. In 1826 at least one hundred U.S. trappers, including seventeen-year-old Kit Carson, received Palace permits.

Spain's iron-fisted economic controls had been bad for business. Colonists needed cheaper merchandise, and foreign traders were eager to provide it. Along with trapping, Mexico legalized foreign trade. Within months, U.S. wagons hit

Kit Carson ca. 1860s.
Courtesy Palace of the
Governors (MNM/DCA)
neg. 58388.

Vial's trail, crammed with goods. Santa Fe Trail trade would determine New Mexico's future.

Anglo-Americans hauled in printed cottons, cutlery, tools, medicines, mirrors, paper, pens, and schoolbooks. They hauled out gold, silver, buffalo hides, furs, woven blankets, and wool. The Old Spanish Trail west became an immigrant route for U.S. families accompanying coast-bound trade caravans. From California came mules and horses. The Camino Real still linked Santa Fe and Mexico City, moving goods, troops, and mail north and south.

As the main market, the Santa Fe Plaza became the major connection for travelers from New Orleans, Saint Louis, Chihuahua, and California. The plaza offered hotels, stables, wagon repair shops, markets, and warehouses, employing many children. The Palace regulated prices, collected freight taxes, distributed mail, and received important visitors.

GOVERNOR NARBONA'S TIME

Governor Antonio Narbona, who served from 1825 to 1827, lived in the Palace with his wife and seven children: Micaela, Francisca, Francisco, Teresa, Mariana, Benigna, and Placido, who ranged in age from twenty-five to one. Their household also included two adult female servants and a seven-year-old male servant. Narbona installed a tall plaza sundial, Santa Fe's only public timepiece. In 1827 incoming Governor Armijo complained that Narbona would not move out so that he could move in.

General Manuel Armijo served three terms as New Mexico's governor beginning in 1827. From a pastel attributed to Alfred S. Waugh in 1846. Courtesy Palace of the Governors (MNM/DCA) neg. 50809.

New Mexicans were starved for services as well as goods. In addition to merchandise, Anglo-Americans brought new ideas and technology. They opened sawmills, flour mills, and distilleries and worked as carpenters, trappers, surveyors, and blacksmiths. American ideas, technology, and goods rapidly gained favor.

GOVERNOR ARMIJO'S REIGN

Governor Manuel Armijo was an experienced administrator and soldier. But incoming Anglo-Americans thought him greedy because he charged high taxes. When Armijo became governor after Pérez's murder, Anglo-Americans found him crafty. When he hosted a Palace ball, Anglo-Americans called him wasteful. When Armijo confronted unlicensed fur trappers in the plaza, Anglo-Americans grabbed their guns. To avoid violence, Armijo backed down, causing Anglo-Americans to think him cowardly as well.

Armijo worried that a few well-armed Anglo-Americans might storm the Palace. When Texas troops threatened just that in 1841, Armijo rode east in challenge. Tricking them into surrendering their weapons, Armijo sent the Texans on foot to Mexico for trial. Anglo-Americans now considered him untrustworthy too.

Armijo tried to reduce government debts and Indian raiding. He gave money for schools and church repair. To fund these projects, Armijo borrowed from Doña Gertrudes Barcelo, or La Tules, who ran a popular gambling casino just off the plaza. While Anglo-Americans objected to loans from a woman of questionable character, they readily borrowed from her later. To please U.S. traders, Armijo lowered taxes, which angered cash-strapped Mexico. Mexican

Brigadier-General Stephen Watts Kearny declared New Mexico as a territory of the United States in 1864. Courtesy Palace of the Governors (MNM/DCA) neg. 9940.

GOVERNOR RECALLED

Governor Mariano Martínez de Lejanza (1844–45) raised taxes on U.S. imports and ignored New Mexico's Indian alliances. As a result, Ute warriors attacked Lejanza in his Palace office. He bravely held the warriors off with a chair while his wife found his sword. Hearing shouts, presidio guards and plaza workmen building a bullring rushed in. Because their leader was killed, the Ute declared war on New Mexico. Lejanza was quickly recalled to Mexico, but not before planting the plaza's cottonwoods.

officials replaced Armijo with Mariano Martínez de Lejanza, but they soon regretted the selection after Lejanza provoked an Indian attack. Armijo then replaced Lejanza for his third and last Palace term (1845–46).

In 1846 the United States declared war on Mexico, forcing New Mexico into a difficult position. Although a Mexican colony, New Mexico depended on U.S. trade. The United States had already annexed Texas and desired California. Under a flag of truce, U.S. agents traveled to Santa Fe, requesting Armijo's peaceful surrender.

The agents reported that Armijo's modest Palace office had homespun rugs on a dirt floor and two calico-covered sofas. They found Armijo, a large

BENT'S FORT

The Bent brothers built a fortified trading post on the Arkansas River in the 1820s. Called the Adobe Castle on the Plains, the fort was short-lived compared to Santa Fe's Palace. As the first territorial governor, Charles Bent left his Adobe Castle for the "Adobe Palace" in 1846.

Charles Bent, the first Anglo-American territorial governor of New Mexico. Courtesy Palace of the Governors (MNM/DCA) neg. 7004.

handsome man, seated at a small table. He wore "a blue frock coat, with a rolling collar and a general's shoulder straps, blue striped 'trowsers' with gold lace, and a red sash" (Hyslop 2002, 330).

It's unclear what actually happened at this meeting. Armijo prepared to block U.S. troops advancing south from Bent's Fort at Apache Canyon east of Santa Fe. Then he suddenly withdrew his men and headed to Mexico City. When U.S. general Stephen Kearny marched into Santa Fe, Governor Armijo was gone.

AMERICAN TERRITORIAL PERIOD

On August 18, 1846, U.S. troops entered the plaza with drawn swords but met no resistance. At the Palace, Colonel Diego Archuleta, left in charge by Armijo, welcomed Kearny's officers with wine and brandy. At sunset, soldiers raised the American flag and fired a plaza salute. Kearny slept on the Palace's earthen floor, declaring U.S. military control the next morning. The U.S. Army continued using the Palace, much as the Spanish and Mexicans had done before. Reports from the time described the Palace without towers and having a printing office at the east end which the Americans continued to use (Shishkin 1972: 27).

To replace the collapsed presidio, soldiers started building Fort Marcy, northeast of the Plaza. Meanwhile, Anglo-Americans and locals attended several Palace balls, where all danced, ate, drank, and smoked. In late September, Kearny headed west, leaving troops, his code of law, and newly appointed governor Charles Bent.

New Mexicans at first believed that Anglo-Americans would claim only the land east of the Rio Grande, next to Texas. But U.S. settlers soon controlled

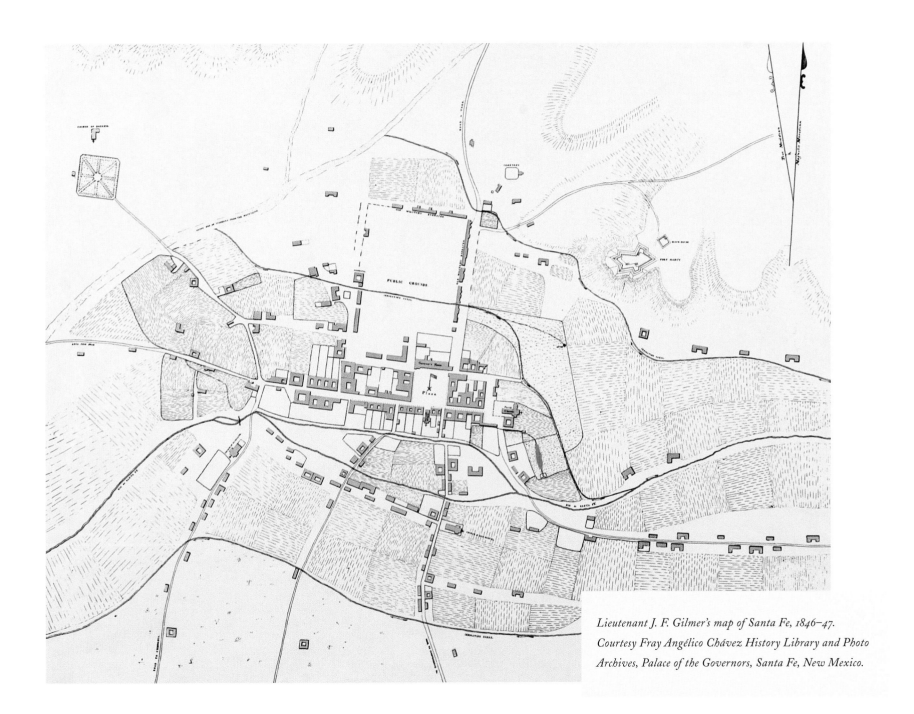

Lieutenant J. F. Gilmer's map of Santa Fe, 1846–47.
Courtesy Fray Angélico Chávez History Library and Photo
Archives, Palace of the Governors, Santa Fe, New Mexico.

Young Meriwether

Teenager David Meriwether accompanied U.S. traders to New Mexico's frontier in 1818. Spanish troops considered Meriwether a spy and jailed him in the Palace for a month. Decades later, Meriwether returned as governor of New Mexico. The evening of his arrival, the roof fell in over his former Palace prison. New Mexicans interpreted the collapse as a favorable omen for his governorship.

lands to the west. Anglo-Americans believed that New Mexicans would appreciate their "liberation" from Mexico. But the local people resented their conquerors' alien laws and sense of racial superiority. New Mexicans also considered Anglo-Americans to be humorless, money-grubbing, and utterly without style. What appeared to be another calm Palace takeover soon broke down. Lack of representation and greed brought violence, continuing the Palace's legacy of rebellion.

TAOS REBELLION: 1847

Discontent with Palace Anglo-Americans grew fast. As with the 1680 and 1837 revolutions, secret plans for territory-wide rebellion took shape. Meanwhile, war with Mexico occupied U.S. and Mexican troops many miles south on the Camino Real.

Governor Bent threw a grand Palace Christmas feast of oysters, shad, preserves, and champagne. The original plot to seize him during dinner had been discovered, so the revolt was rescheduled for January 1847. When Bent rode home to Taos to move his wife and children to the Palace, rebels scalped him in front of his family.

Meanwhile, U.S. soldiers encountered uprisings throughout the northern valleys. Among the resistors was Diego Archuleta, who had met Kearney at the Palace after Armijo had fled. The revolt continued until Mexico surrendered to the United States in 1848. Once New Mexico was unquestionably part of the United States, its freedom fighters fled to Mexico.

New Mexico became a U.S. territory, its governor and important officials appointed by the U.S. president. Visiting Pueblo representatives were still provided Palace meals and a room to stay. However, "liberation" excluded both Indians and women, denied full rights as citizens for decades to come.

Territorial officers occupied the Palace, but after three assassinated governors in twelve years (Pérez, González, and Bent), few felt safe. In 1851 Secretary John Greiner wrote, "Here I am in the Palace of Santa Fe. . . . If I succeed in getting safely back to my friends under Providence I shall consider myself a highly favored man!" (Kenner 1969, 119n).

Governor David Meriwether, who served from 1853 to 1856, hosted many Palace visitors, including Ute chief Tamouche, his wife, and Comanches reporting Osage attacks. Like earlier Spanish governors, Meriwether handled witchcraft cases. In 1854 at the Palace, Meriwether tried several Nambe Indians who had killed a local "witch." Meriwether also returned Mexican slave children found in New Mexico.

RAIDING RETURNS

Like Mexico, the United States did not honor Governor Anza's peace alliances. By 1850 Anglo-Americans had ruined any remaining Comanche, Ute, Navajo, and Apache treaties. While Spain had discouraged raiding with gifts and supplies, the United States offered only military might.

Raiding became a major political issue. In 1849 Apaches killed five Santa Fe Trail merchants, capturing a Mrs. White and her young daughter. Despite large rewards, the two disappeared. Governor Calhoun James (1851–52) proposed evacuating all Santa Fe women and children since raiding was so fierce. The Palace supplied guns and ammunition to citizen posses and Pueblo troops for self-defense.

MANUELITO

In 1834, when Navajo warrior Manuelito was sixteen, he married Chief Narbona's daughter. He accompanied Narbona to unsuccessful Palace peace talks and helped defeat Pérez in the winter of 1835 at the Battle of Copper Pass. In 1846 Manuelito signed the Treaty of Ojo del Oso with the United States. Territorial governor David Meriwether appointed Manuelito "official Navajo spokesman," awarding him a cane and a medal. But settlers continued hostilities, so Manuelito renewed his attacks. Manuelito's band avoided capture until 1866. The U.S. Army marched him through the plaza to prove it had overpowered this famous resistor.

Doña Tules (Gertrudes Barcelo), Santa Fe's infamous saloon keeper. From Harpers Monthly Magazine, *April 1854, courtesy Palace of the Governors (MNM/DCA) neg. 50815.*

Santa Fe gamblers at the casino of Doña Tules.

TRADE

Territorial Santa Fe capitalized on its key economic position. Trail trade boomed, mail and stage lines expanded, and the plaza remained a vibrant marketplace. Merchants prospered from army contracts for wool, meat, and hides. Traffic across the plains increased with California-bound settlers and gold seekers. On the trail going west, plaza stores were the last chance for supplies.

The plaza market served locals too. Vendors offered produce, venison, turkey, and butchered mutton under the plaza's cottonwoods. Pueblo Indians sold pottery, corn, melons, woven rugs, beadwork, jewelry, baskets, and silver-trimmed saddles. Citizens celebrated freight wagon arrival with dances held in front of the Palace. As trader Josiah Gregg observed, "Nothing is more general, throughout the country, and with all classes, than dancing" (Padilla 1992). Locals also enjoyed plaza concerts, bullfights, fiestas, processions, and folk dramas.

Elsberg–Amberg wagon train on the plaza, October 1861. Courtesy Palace of the Governors (MNM/DCA) neg. 11254.

Black military musicians of the Ninth Cavalry Band play in the plaza, July 1880. Photo by Ben Wittick, courtesy Palace of the Governors (MNM/DCA) neg. 50887.

Despite failed alliances and legalized foreign commerce, Comanchero trade continued. Comancheros often served double duty—trading as well as reporting to the Palace on Plains Indian activities. Occasionally they located and ransomed hostages. In 1850 a twelve-year-old boy was redeemed with tobacco, corn, blankets, knives, and red cloth. Another boy, the same age, cost one horse, a shirt, pants, a rifle, powder and bullets, and a buffalo robe.

THE EARLY TERRITORIAL PALACE: 1850–80

When Kearny invaded Santa Fe, the Royal Palace had already served ten generations of New Mexicans. What the Anglo-Americans now simply called the Adobe Palace was the only building in town with glass windows. At 350 feet, 25 percent longer than it is today, the single-story Palace extended across what is now Lincoln Street. In addition to Fort Marcy, soldiers used the presidio ruins attached to the Palace, but no other casas reales structures remained.

While some Anglo-Americans viewed the Palace as "suitable to the dignity of a governor of New Mexico," others found it barbaric. Its east and west ends had caved in, offering little security. Nonetheless, Anglo-Americans held with tradition, adapting the Palace for their own use. A theater eventually replaced the old ballroom, and remodeled colonial offices housed territorial assemblies.

In 1851 several east Palace rooms became a library, housing more than two thousand law books and manuscripts. Governors used central Palace rooms for living and office space. By the mid-1850s, a Territorial-style porch graced the Palace entrance facing south. West rooms included the Indian Agency, Indian visiting quarters, a jail, and a guardhouse.

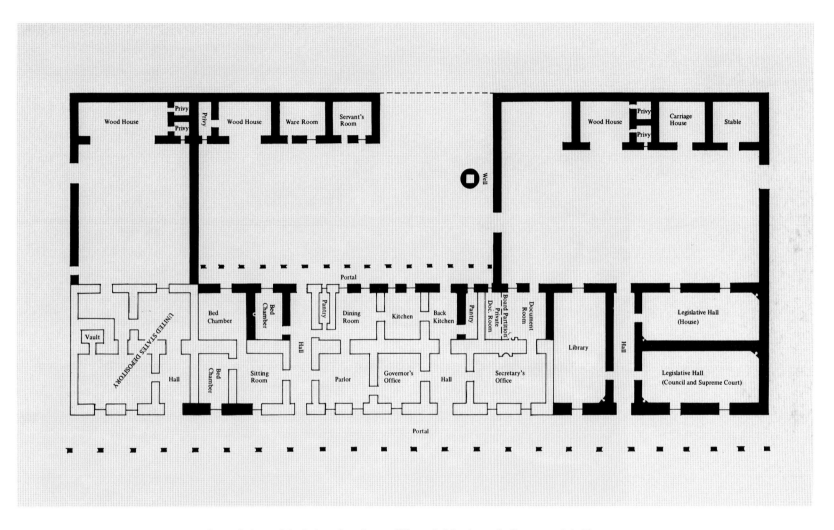

Ground plans of the Palace, from letter of Henry S. Martin to the Secretary of the Treasury, Jan. 16, 1869. Courtesy National Archives.

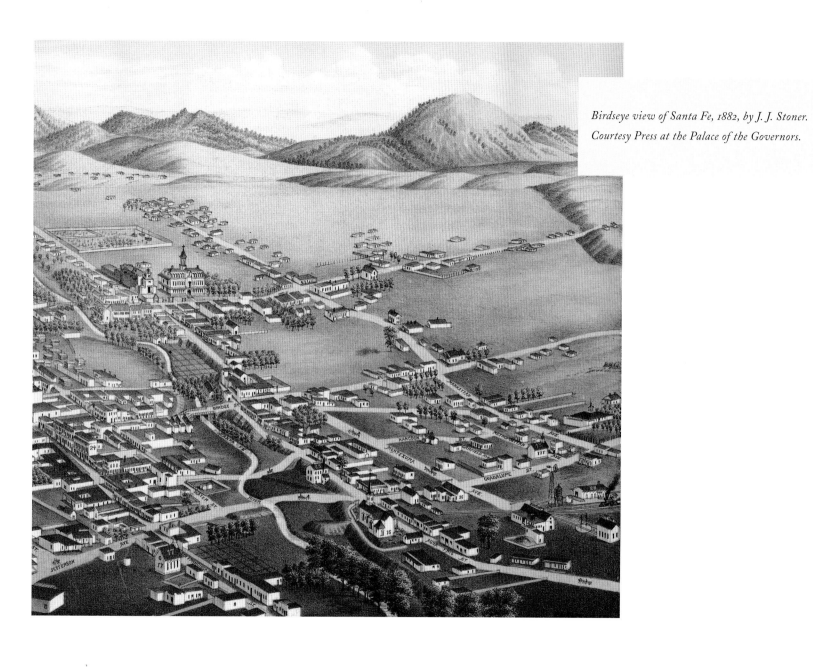

Birdseye view of Santa Fe, 1882, by J. J. Stoner.
Courtesy Press at the Palace of the Governors.

Navajos in Santa Fe, circa 1870, discuss a truce with Comanches who were raiding the Bosque Redondo reservation. From an illustration by Bell, 1870.

CIVIL WAR YEARS

During the Civil War, most New Mexicans were Union supporters—their loyalty forged through trade and a general distrust of Texas. The Confederates, however, wanted California gold, and New Mexico was in the way. Confederate troops captured El Paso in 1861 and moved north up the Camino Real.

Citizen forces failed to keep Confederates from occupying Albuquerque. Governor Henry Connelly abandoned the Palace and fled to Fort Union near Las Vegas. Confederates took over the Palace and continued east on the Santa Fe Trail.

Union troops gathering at Fort Union marched west, facing the enemy at Glorieta Pass in March 1862. Meanwhile, civilian volunteers trapped the Southern invaders from behind. By April the Confederates had abandoned the Palace, leaving only champagne bottles. New Mexicans chased the Confederates back down the Camino Real, defeating them near Peralta.

President Abraham Lincoln awarded silver-headed canes to Pueblo governors for their loyalty and loans to pay Union salaries. Black bunting draped the Palace, marking Lincoln's assassination in 1865. (Today a Plaza monument commemorates those lost in New Mexico's Civil War battles.)

Meanwhile, Apache and Navajo raiding increased. The U.S. Army issued warnings before moving in to punish and remove groups to government-controlled reservations, where Indians were supposed to learn about Christianity and farming. In 1865 defeated Navajo families walked east to reservation lands on the Pecos River, joining captured Apache bands. The "Long Walk" proved disastrous in every way. In 1873 surviving Navajos returned west, to reservation lands carved from their former territories.

THE LATE TERRITORIAL PALACE

Constantly needing repair, the Palace was updated after the war. Lincoln Street replaced much of the Palace's collapsed west end. A new stone jail was completed near Fort Marcy. Presidio ruins were flattened to clear space for houses and businesses.

Now flanked by Lincoln Street, west Palace rooms housed the U.S. Depository, which safeguarded government funds. In June 1869, a young Palace servant girl discovered the body of a depository worker, Colonel J. L. Collins, a bullet in his chest. At least $100,000 was missing.

The Palace in an 1884 etching by William Ritch. Courtesy Palace of the Governors (MNM/DCA) neg. 011212.

LEW WALLACE

Lew Wallace's life was filled with adventure. At age five he saved his younger brother from being crushed by carriage wheels. After surviving scarlet fever, Wallace spent much of his childhood reading, drawing, hunting, and avoiding school. At age thirteen, he ran away for twelve days with Harrison-for-President campaigners. He played violin, devoured his father's library of books, and started writing historical novels at sixteen. Wallace served in the Mexican War and was later one of the youngest generals in the Union army. After his eventful term as New Mexico's governor, Wallace was appointed U.S. minister to Turkey.

Gov. Lew. Wallace, 1886. Engraving after a photograph by Napoleon Sarony. From Harper's Weekly Magazine. *Courtesy Palace of the Governors (MNM/DCA) neg. 13123.*

Billy the Kid & Governor Wallace

The Lincoln County War marked Lew Wallace's term as governor. While this range feud occurred in the south, teenage ringleader Billy the Kid supposedly vowed: "I mean to ride up to the plaza at Santa Fe, hitch my horse in front of the Palace, and put a bullet through Lew Wallace" (Weigle and White 1988, 154). Friends suggested latching Palace shutters at night "so the bright light of the student's lamp might not make such a shining mark of the governor writing until late" (Chauvenet 1983, 68). Wallace did not volunteer for a second term.

Susan E. Wallace

Susan Elston grew up in Indiana, married Lew Wallace in 1852, and had a son, Henry, in 1856. With Henry grown, Lew moved to the Palace during his governorship. Susan eventually joined him. Like her husband, Susan was the author of several books. Perhaps her most famous was *In the Land of the Pueblos*, a history of New Mexico published in 1888, which helped launch and popularize a regional literature of the Southwest. In his autobiography, Lew wrote of Susan: "What I have of success, all that I am, is owing to her." Susan died in 1907.

Most Anglo-Americans by then viewed the Palace as old-fashioned and foreign. They masked its poor condition with Victorian architecture and decorations. Planks covered dirt floors, tacked-up cloth disguised sagging ceilings, and wallpaper hid cracked plaster. Hoping to replace territorial status with statehood, New Mexicans wanted a more progressive, "American" look. Embarrassingly dingy, the Palace was considered quaint at best.

New doors, shuttered glass windows, chimneys, and wood walkways under the portal were installed. But the Palace really needed a new roof. The existing five-foot-thick earthen structure let in plenty of rain. Describing the roof's decayed timbers and immense weight, Governor Marsh Giddings wrote: "We are living every hour in or beneath a perfect dead fall" (Shishkin 1968, 35). In 1877 the Palace exterior was whitewashed and painted with imitation blocks. It received a fancy Victorian portal the following year.

Territorial governor Lew Wallace, who served from 1878 to 1881, completed his famous novel *Ben Hur* in his Palace study. He wrote, "The ghosts, if they were about, did not disturb me; yet in the hush of that gloomy room, I beheld the Crucifixion and strove to write what I beheld" (Weigle and White 1988, 154). His best seller eventually became a popular Hollywood film. Wallace's Palace office later became known as the Ben Hur Room.

The railroad arrived in New Mexico in 1880, ending sixty years of Santa Fe Trail trade. From Las Vegas, the tracks detoured south, straight to Albuquerque, with only a small spur line connecting to Santa Fe. In losing commercial control, Santa Fe lost cultural and political influence too. A modern capitol building, "worthy of statehood," was built off the plaza. However, the Palace remained the governor's residence and office, at least for a time.

Engraving from a pencil sketch of the Palace in 1889 by Gov. Lew. Wallace (1827–1905).

Courtesy Palace of the Governors (MNM/DCA).

Santa Fe Plaza, ca. 1887, looking north toward the Palace. Courtesy Palace of the Governors (MNM/DCA) neg. 11299.

Oñaté Trail, Leading North

Presbyterian Church.   Hospital.

Baldy Peak.   Santa Fe Range.   Cañon of the Rio Santa Fe.

Santa Fe Academy.   The Fort.

Soldiers' Barracks.   H'dq'rs of the Post.   Palace Hotel.   Old Spanish Government Palace.

Officers' Quarters.   Officers' Quarters.   Residence of Gen. L. P. Bradley, Com'dg Dist.

Grant Street, looking North.   Palace Avenue, looking East.   General Offices.

The further of the three residences facing Grant Street was the quarters of Ex-President Grant and family, when they visited Santa Fe, in 1880.

Headquarters, Military District of New Mexico (Fort Marcy) looking southeast, ca. 1885.
The Palace of the Governors is at extreme right. The open area west of the Palace was the real
center of military life at the time. From Illustrated New Mexico, *by William G. Ritch,*
courtesy Palace of the Governors (MNM/DCA) neg. 1738.

Corpus Christi procession in front of the Palace, ca. 1870–74. Photo by H. T. Hiester, courtesy Palace of the Governors (MNM/DCA) neg. 38022.

Plaza in front of Palace, ca. 1866–68, looking east, a center of life in Santa Fe through the ages. Photo by Nicholas Brown, courtesy Palace of the Governors (MNM/DCA) neg. 38025.

Interior hallway, Palace of the Governors, Feb. 14, 1893. Photo by Thomas J. Curran,
courtesy Palace of the Governors (MNM/DCA) neg. 46776.

Ben Hur Room at the Palace, courtesy Palace of the Governors (MNM/DCA) neg. 16660.

Interior of Palace post office. Courtesy Palace of the Governors (MNM/DCA) neg. 16659.

Palace parlor during Ross administration, 1880s. Photo by D. B. Chase, courtesy Palace of the Governors (MNM/DCA) neg. 67249.

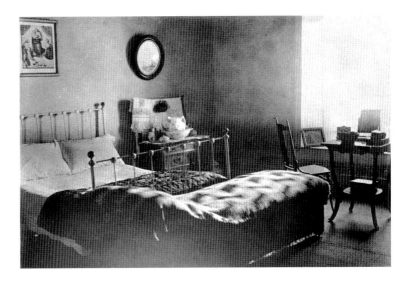

Governor Lew. Wallace bedroom. Courtesy Palace of the Governors (MNM/DCA) neg. 12175.

Dining Room during Prince administration, Feb. 14, 1893. Photo by Thomas J. Curran, courtesy Palace of the Governors (MNM/DCA) neg. 46775.

The governor's son, Miguel Otero Jr., has a birthday party, ca. 1899–1900. Photo by P. H. Weitfle, courtesy Palace of the Governors (MNM/DCA) neg. 25569.

*Governor Prince's parlor, Feb. 14, 1893. Son William
is seated far left. Photo by Thomas J. Curran, courtesy
Palace of the Governors (MNM/DCA) neg. 46774.*

PRINCE

During Governor L. Bradford Prince's administration (1889–93), the Palace was about 254 feet long. The western forty-three feet housed the post office and a bank. The next one hundred feet included the governor's offices and residence and reception rooms. Army offices filled the next twenty-seven-foot section. The New Mexico Historical Society museum shared the Palace's eastern end with the library. The society collected historic and Indian artifacts, geological specimens, curiosities, maps, and historic documents.

Among the first to appreciate New Mexico's rich cultural history, symbolized by the Palace, Prince was committed to its preservation. Prince, his wife, and their young son William were Palace residents and often received guests. (Prince's Victorian parlor has been re-created in the modern Palace museum. It displays Prince's fossil and Native pottery collections.)

According to 1890s newspapers, repairs during Prince's term greatly enhanced Palace appearances. "Unsightly cornices" were removed; the roof replaced; and hard plaster and paint applied inside and out. The new sidewalk installed along the portal was a "joy forever." The Palace was "overhauled and modernized just enough to show what can be done with an 'old adobe' house while at the same time preserving many of those characteristics which serve to make this structure full of romantic interest to people from all parts of the country" (Shishkin 972: 46).

OTERO: 1897–1906

Governor Miguel A. Otero didn't live in the Palace but he kept his offices there. As more government meetings occurred at the new capitol, the Palace's role came into question. Because the territorial government could not afford the constant upkeep, Otero tried unsuccessfully to donate the Palace to the Smithsonian Institution.

In the fall of 1897, Pueblo governors visited the Palace for a traditional new-governor meeting. Many brought interpreters and President Lincoln's silver-headed canes. Most likely, Otero's son Miguel, then about five, was there too. All gathered later at the Otero home for chocolate and cake.

In 1898 the United States declared war on Spain. Although Washington, D.C., repeatedly denied New Mexico's statehood requests, it expected the territory to provide soldiers. Otero mustered four units of mounted Rough Riders in the plaza. This willingness to serve later helped New Mexico acquire statehood. Young Miguel certainly cheered on the recruits from the Palace portal.

In the early 1900s, fewer governors lived in the Palace. The New Mexico Historical Society still used the Palace's eastern rooms, while the west end housed the post office. Territorial funds could not cover Palace repair costs. No one knew what to do with the shabby, hard-to-maintain old structure.

In 1907 officials scrambled to remodel central Palace rooms to house Governor George Curry. A former Rough Rider, Curry was the last governor to live in the Palace, three centuries after Peralta. Curry's three teenage sons likely visited from the family home in Las Cruces. During Curry's term, the road between Santa Fe and Albuquerque, part of the Camino Real, was improved. The upgrade included cutting a roadway through La Bajada Hill.

The Palace was almost three hundred, and its future looked bleak. Who would pay for upkeep? Some suggested selling the Palace to the highest bidder. The new capitol and government buildings better reflected New Mexico's modern status as a statehood candidate. But there was life in the old Palace yet.

GROWING UP IN THE PALACE

The younger Miguel Otero accompanied his father around New Mexico and outside the state. In 1899, at age six or seven, he met prisoner Tom "Black Jack" Ketchum, a notorious train robber. Miguel took Tom some peanuts and pleaded for his release, but Ketchum was later tried and hanged. A few years later, a rabid dog bit Miguel. He dutifully submitted to the painful "Pasteur cure," involving thirty stomach injections. When Miguel was about twelve, his father's political enemies plotted to kidnap him. Fortunately, the plot was discovered, and Miguel was unharmed.

Gov. Miguel A. Otero. Photo by Prince Studio, courtesy Palace of the Governors (MNM/DCA) neg. 50609.

Territorial Governor Miguel A. Otero's inauguration parade, June 14, 1897. Photo by
P. E. Harroun, courtesy Palace of the Governors (MNM/DCA) neg. 14090.

Military group in front of Palace, ca. 1890–1900. Courtesy Palace of the Governors
(MNM/DCA) neg. 47821.

Edgar L. Hewett and field trip in front of Palace, ca. 1915. Courtesy Palace of the Governors (MNM/DCA) neg. 14234.

1909–2009

A Century of Innovation

After decades of struggle, New Mexico finally won statehood in 1912. As state laws replaced territorial laws, the capitol building officially replaced the sagging Palace as New Mexico's government seat.

Alarmed by talk of the Palace's pending sale and likely destruction, historically minded locals created the Museum of New Mexico Association in 1909. That same year, the new Museum of New Mexico took over the Palace. After three hundred years of service as a government, military, and cultural center, the Palace would serve a new function. The building where so much history had happened would no longer stage that history but would showcase it for future generations.

The Palace had narrowly escaped demolition, proving it had not outlived public usefulness. As it turned three hundred, the venerable building became an art and history museum. Built three centuries before to represent and broadcast Spanish culture, the palace-turned-museum would now represent and broadcast

1909/10... **The Palace** turns three hundred

1912...... **New Mexico** becomes the forty-seventh U.S. state

1909–13... **The Palace is remodeled** and turned into a museum

1917...... **The Fine Arts Museum** is built over the former royal presidio; the United States enters World War I

1941...... **The Japanese** attack Pearl Harbor

1974–75... **Archaeologist Cordelia Snow** leads excavations at the Palace

1980...... **New Mexico marks** the three hundredth anniversary of the Pueblo Revolt

2003...... **Archaeologist Steve Post** and team carry out excavations north of the Palace

2009..... **A new history museum** opens adjacent to the Palace

Edgar L. Hewett, first Museum of New
Mexico director, 1911, San Diego,
California, ca. 1932. Photo by Jack Adams,
courtesy Palace of the Governors
(MNM/DCA) neg. 7373.

Edgar L. Hewett, second from right, in the
Palace courtyard, Fiestas, August 2–5, 1925.
Courtesy Palace of the Governors
(MNM/DCA).

New Mexican culture. Archaeologist Edgar Lee Hewett became the museum's first director.

The plaza, meanwhile, had lost command as a trade center. But thanks to the adaptable city of Santa Fe, it regained commercial and cultural influence. Passenger trains traveled up the small spur line to Santa Fe's station southwest of the plaza. Eastern visitors found the flat-roofed adobe buildings around the open plaza curious and appealing. Soon the plaza exchanged its outdated economy for a new, vital tourist industry based on an exotic history. The three-hundred-year-old Palace—the very image of this picturesque past—led the way.

The palace/museum transformed the fading plaza into an international market for Indian jewelry and crafts. Together, the Palace and plaza regained

Palace of the Governors, ca. 1914–16. Photo by Jesse Nusbaum, courtesy Palace of the Governors (MNM/DCA) neg. 139153.

Model Ts on the Plaza at Palace ca. 1915. Photo by George L. Beam, courtesy Palace of the Governors (MNM/DCA) neg. 6850.

Palace patio artists, 1917. Courtesy Palace of the Governors (MNM/DCA) neg. 13325.

cultural clout, determining architectural style, encouraging art and commerce, and promoting pride in New Mexico's past.

THE PALACE BECOMES A MUSEUM

As always, the Palace needed remodeling. Just as Pueblo rebels had revamped the Palace for their needs, and later colonists had added a new presidio, the structure required extensive repairs and adjustments. In 1909 the Museum of New Mexico hired university instructor and archaeologist Jesse Nusbaum to do the job.

Nusbaum's "restoration" actually proved historically destructive. However, without his replacing rotten vigas (log beams), removing water-soaked walls, and installing new flooring, the Palace would have soon collapsed. By enlarging

rooms and adding modern heating, lights, and display cases, Nusbaum turned the Palace into the Museum of the Palace of the Governors. It would be a public cultural attraction, and visitor fees would pay for upkeep. The new museum would jumpstart New Mexico's history as a new state while honoring its colorful colonial and territorial past.

The rebuilt Palace looked much as it does today. Claiming to stay true to the Palace's past, Nusbaum, in fact, had few historical guidelines. There were no photos, sketches, or detailed accounts of the palace prior to the U.S. conquest. Nusbaum's "Spanish colonial look" (Wilson 1997: 126) existed primarily in the minds of town boosters. If anything, the new museum looked more Pueblo than Spanish. Nusbaum's desire for a serviceable and imposing structure also governed

Vendors under Palace portal, mid-1930s. Photo by T. Harmon Parkhurst, mid-1930s, courtesy Palace of the Governors (MNM/DCA) neg. 69973.

Julian and María Martínez and family on the Palace portal ca. 1929. Courtesy Palace of the Governors (MNM/DCA) neg. 164605.

When the Circus Came to Santa Fe, ca. 1915–20. Photo by Sheldon Parsons, courtesy Palace of the Governors (MNM/DCA) neg. 191768.

Hay haulers in plaza, ca. 1913. Photo by Jesse Nusbaum, courtesy Palace of the Governors (MNM/DCA) neg. 61545.

his vision. As a result, the new Palace became a model for a "Santa Fe style" based more on nostalgia for the past than on careful historical research.

The new Palace included archaeology labs and art studios. The first museum exhibit, held in 1912, displayed photos of southwestern architecture, comparing Santa Fe and California Mission styles. Carl Lotave painted murals on Palace walls. The images honored New Mexico's diverse history and peoples, including prehistoric Pueblo communities on nearby Pajarito Plateau.

In 1915 Santa Fe architects won an award at the San Diego Pacific Exposition for a building design combining features from Acoma and other New Mexico missions. The award prompted plaza builders to celebrate, not suppress, adobe architecture. They created a unified, if imaginary, architectural setting for tourists to experience New Mexico's past. The resulting mythical Santa Fe style promoted tourism and transformed the plaza from a frontier outpost into a national cultural icon. City planners dedicated both Palace and plaza to marketing historic New Mexico.

The museum introduced the *Journal of the Museum of New Mexico* in 1913. Renamed *El Palacio*, it is the oldest museum journal in the United States. The popular magazine chronicles New Mexico's remarkable heritage of art, culture, history, archaeology, and environment.

FINE ARTS MUSEUM

The museum exhibited art at the Palace until the new Fine Arts Museum opened in 1917, off the northwest corner of the plaza. Artistic expression of all kinds has been and remains central to New Mexico's diverse culture. New Mexicans needed a museum for history and for arts. "Whether painting, writing, or weaving their experiences, New Mexicans have made history and the arts elements of everyday living" (Meadows 1984, 33). This second museum made few attempts to incorporate the royal presidio ruins on which it stood, instead promoting the plaza's new look. The Palace was now the only remnant left of Peralta's casas reales.

During Fine Arts Museum construction, workers uncovered a skeleton with a turquoise and abalone shell necklace. An arrowhead, still embedded, had shattered the person's spine. Workers found more human skeletons, plus pottery shards and buffalo, wildcat, and bighorn sheep bones. New Mexico's history, often violent, had happened right there.

The Fine Arts Museum celebrated southwestern, Spanish, Anglo, and Native American artists. It also helped elevate Indian crafts to a recognized art form. Like the old Palace, the museum's auditorium hosted public events. Citizens attended receptions, high school graduations, concerts, lectures, and theater productions there.

PLAZA

After the railroad bypassed Santa Fe, plaza trade had shrunk to include only local sellers of firewood, produce, wool, and livestock. The two plaza museums, however, introduced a new appreciation and market for Indian and folk art. A thriving art market developed in front of the Palace. The open-ended portals encouraged foot traffic, while the southern orientation offered winter warmth and summer protection from the sun. Visitors eagerly bought Pueblo pottery and Navajo silver, beadwork, and woven rugs from portal vendors.

Soon Santa Fe–style craft and curio shops replaced older downtown buildings. Like the old presidio, these stores surrounded the new museums and plaza, creating an exotic commercial environment. Through it all, the Palace and plaza

MARÍA MARTÍNEZ

During the early 1900s, Museum of New Mexico archaeologists encouraged Indians to sell their wares at the Palace of the Governors. Potter María Martínez, from San Ildefonso Pueblo, made exceptional Black-on-black ware decorated by her husband, Julian, until his death in 1943. María's pottery linked the discoveries of archaeologists working on ancestral Puebloan lands with the emerging world of twentieth-century Native American art. An artist of international stature, María Martínez's pottery helped revive and elevate southwestern pottery to an art form and valued livelihood.

María Martínez in the patio of the Palace, ca. 1915. Photo by T. Harmon Parkhurst, courtesy Palace of the Governors (MNM/DCA) neg. 42317.

Presentation of the Flags of the Allied Powers at Victory and Peace Festival during Fiesta,
ca. 1919. Photo by Wesley Bradfield, courtesy Palace of the Governors (MNM/DCA) neg. 52394.

De Vargas Pageant, ca. 1911. Photo by Jesse Nusbaum, courtesy Palace of the Governors (MNM/DCA) neg. 10801.

Burning of Zozobra, Fiesta, 1995. Photo by Mark Nohl.

remained centers for cross-cultural interaction. Residents still strolled the plaza—always the local social hub—to meet friends and hear news. Bands played, parades gathered, and Pueblo dancers performed. The two museums contributed, hosting puppet shows and arts fairs.

In the 1920s the Spanish Colonial Art Society formed to promote Hispanic arts. The plaza's annual Spanish Colonial Arts Market soon developed, encouraging Hispanic artists to make and sell traditional items: woodcarvings, tinwork, wool embroidery, weavings, and foods.

PALACE LIBRARY

The Fray Angélico Chávez History Library continued the Palace's library legacy, in place since Governor Vargas's time. Territorial manuscripts later greatly expanded Palace holdings. Located on the Palace's east end, today's collections include more than fifty thousand books, five hundred linear feet of archives, and seven thousand maps. The library owns an original copy of Gaspar Pérez de Villagrá's epic *La Historia de la Nueva Mexico,* published in 1610. Also present are Mexican-era volumes, Kearny's code of territorial law, books owned by Governor Lew Wallace, rare maps, WPA files, and a vast historical photo archive.

PALACE PRINTING

The Palace once housed New Mexico's first printing press, transported over the Santa Fe Trail. That same press printed two Mexican-era newspapers, *La Verdad* and *El Payo de Nuevo Mejico.* Anglo-Americans printed Kearny's code, followed by a newspaper, the *Santa Fe Republican,* from 1846 through 1848.

The Print Shop at the Palace of the Governors, photo by Blair Clark.

The Palace continues this printing heritage through its print shop and bindery, established in the late 1960s. The Press at the Palace of the Governors produces high-quality letterpress limited-edition books and promotes traditional hand-crafted book arts and printing history. The program includes a large research library, several nineteenth-century presses and tools, hundreds of type fonts, and a book bindery. Printed newspaper headlines displayed from New Mexico's historical newspaper-publishing past chronicle much territorial history: Civil War battles, Indian raids, and "wanted" posters.

MUSIC IN THE PLAZA

The Santa Fe Concert Band played Sunday concerts from the plaza's bandstand throughout the mid-1900s. The band also played for the annual Fiesta, escorting processions around the plaza. The band broke up with the start of World War II and played its last Fiesta in 1939. Various plaza bands performed afterward. In 1983 the Santa Fe Concert Band re-formed, and it continues the tradition of Fiesta and occasional plaza concerts.

Corpus Christi Procession, Santa Fe, June 1942. Photo New Mexico State Tourist Bureau, courtesy Palace of the Governors (MNM/DCA) neg. 144801.

TRICENTENNIAL OF THE PUEBLO REVOLT

New Mexican Indians commemorated the three-hundredth anniversary of the Pueblo Revolt in August 1980 with a five-day tricentennial run. Modern participants honored ancient Native American running traditions employed by the original revolt runners. Starting at Taos, Indian runners raced to Tesuque, Santa Fe, and many Pueblo towns, ending at Hopi and Zuni. The tricentennial run offered New Mexicans an opportunity to reconsider the role of the conquest and forced assimilation. Resistance and running remain important to Pueblo identity.

Archaeologist Marge Lambert directs excavations in the Palace patio, 1956. Photo by Art Taylor, courtesy Palace of the Governors (MNM/DCA) neg. 6821.

BEST AND BIGGEST ARTIFACT

In 1960 both Palace and plaza received recognition as National Historic Landmarks. The honor emphasized the importance of southwestern events that had occurred in our nation's East Coast–oriented history. Such landmarks have national, not just regional, meaning for all Americans. They belong to the public, help form bonds between people, and invite everyone to feel connection with our national past. As a testament to their importance as historic landmarks, the plaza and Palace host more than one hundred thousand visitors annually. They sponsor major public events attracting thousands more.

Since the 1970s, archaeologists have studied the Palace as a living artifact. In anticipation of much-needed repairs, Laboratory of Anthropology archaeologist Cordelia Snow excavated several interior Palace rooms in 1974. Snow removed the wooden floors in what are now known as Room 5 and Room 7. She found that these rooms had been very different in previous centuries.

Snow's findings were architecturally complex. They included wall foundations at different levels and massive footings for multiple stories. The area dug may have once been a passageway. Nine revolt-era (1680–92) pits, probably used for food storage, were also uncovered. Post-revolt trash included trout bones, likely from the Santa Fe River. Snow also located many seventeenth-century artifacts, including Pueblo pottery, Spanish maiolica, and Chinese porcelain shards. Some of the shards had been reworked into spindle whorls. An excavated Chinese porcelain cup, a glass earring, hand-blown glass, pins, needles, buttons, and a bone ring are currently displayed in the Palace. Room 5 test pit revealed layers of adobe brick floors. The earliest, dating from 1640 to 1680, had a diagonal pattern, rare in New Mexico.

In 1982 laboratory archaeologist Curt Schaafsma excavated outside the Palace's north side, where a new bank and offices were to be built. This area was probably part of Anza's 1791 presidio courtyard and possibly part of the earlier Palace. Schaafsma's crew found traces of Anza's presidio walls and eighteenth-century pottery shards, stone tools, and animal bones. Glass bottles and metal artifacts represented the Civil War years.

In 2003 and 2006, laboratory archaeologist Steve Post headed two excavation seasons to further study the Palace's exterior. This research was undertaken

Replica of a pre-revolt-era (mid 1600s) earring uncovered by archaeologists inside the Palace's western rooms during 1974-75 excavations. Photo by Tony Grant, Santa Cruz, CA.

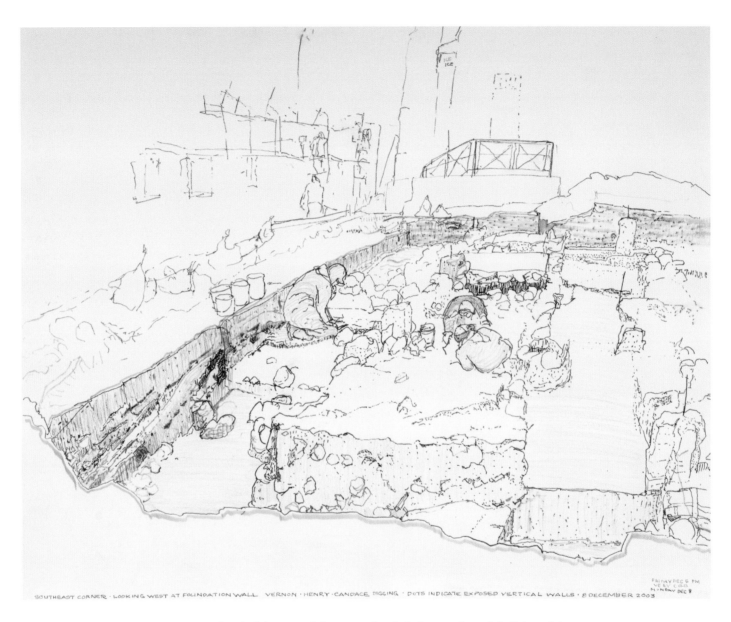

SOUTHEAST CORNER · LOOKING WEST AT FOUNDATION WALL   VERNON · HENRY · CANDACE DIGGING · DOTS INDICATE EXPOSED VERTICAL WALLS · 8 DECEMBER 2003

Artist Carol Stanford documented the 2003 archaeological excavations of the Palace of the Governors. Southwest corner, looking west at foundation wall.

Below: Archaeologist Jessica Badner recording cobble foundation below the Palace of the Governors Print Shop. Palace excavation, 2003, courtesy Office of Archaeological Studies, Museum of New Mexico.

Excavation of Structure 2 cobble foundation. Structure 2 was one of the eighteenth-century buildings investigated by the 2003 field project. Photo by Carol Price, courtesy Office of Archaeological Studies, Museum of New Mexico.

SEGESSER HIDE PAINTING

In 1988 the Museum of New Mexico bought two large paintings on sewn buffalo hides. Created by an unknown eyewitness, the frantic scenes depict warring Spanish, Pueblo, Plains, and French troops. The battle is Pedro de Villasur's fatal last stand, launched from the Palace in 1720. After their creation, the hides mysteriously came into the possession of a Sonoran missionary, Felipe Van Segesser, who shipped them home to his family in Switzerland in 1758. Two centuries later, Van Segesser family members contacted the Palace about shipping these colorful and detailed artworks home. The Segesser Hide Paintings are now displayed at the Palace.

Detail from Segesser Hide Painting.

in preparation for a new history museum to be built north of the Palace. Post found three foundation layers. The top and most recent layer dated to the mid-1800s. The middle foundation was from the late seventeenth to early eighteenth century. This construction remnant may represent Governor Cubero's Palace restoration efforts after the reconquest. The lowest and oldest wall footing was possibly from the pueblo/palace or prerevolt Palace. Post also found a late-eighteenth-century trash pit, possibly linked to Anza's 1791 presidio construction.

TWENTIETH-CENTURY ACCOMPLISHMENTS

Throughout the later 1900s, the Museum of New Mexico system added more museums beyond the plaza's Palace of the Governors and Museum of Fine Arts. In 1953 the Museum of International Folk Art opened on Camino Lejo to join the Laboratory of Anthropology, a research institute that became part of the Museum of New Mexico in 1947, followed in 1987 by the Museum of Indian Arts and Culture. Along with two private museums these now form the area known as Museum Hill.

The Museum of New Mexico's newest addition, the New Mexico History Museum, will open in 2009 to coincide with the Palace's four-hundredth anniversary. Located to the Palace's north boundary, the three-story museum will stand on what was once part of Anza's presidio and possibly earlier casas reales structures. It will include twenty thousand square feet of exhibit space for historical artifacts, photographic and painted images, and maps.

The new history museum will address New Mexican regional history, allowing the current Palace to adjust its focus to its own historic artifact displays and interpretation. An artifact itself, the Palace remains a powerful symbol of cultural influence, violence, and fusion. The newly organized Palace will celebrate

Architectural rendering for new History Museum of New Mexico in Santa Fe.
Courtesy Conron & Woods Architects, Santa Fe, New Mexico.

the unique heritage created by New Mexico's cultural groups through four centuries of interaction occurring right at the Palace and plaza.

The year 2009 will mark the Palace's four hundredth anniversary—with three hundred of those years spent as New Mexico's government residence and capitol, plus one hundred years as a museum and cultural center. As it nears the anniversary, the Palace will again change to better serve New Mexico's public, taking on a new museum role alongside New Mexico's new historical museum.

The courtyard of the Palace. Drawing by Carol Stanford, 2004.

2009–2109

A CENTURY of ANTICIPATION

Continuously repaired and remodeled over four centuries, the Palace of the Governors reflects the nature of its construction materials (wood construction would allow different design possibilities and require different repairs and remodels; adobe and viga construction dictates wall thickness, width of rooms, and height of building) and needs of the times. Through it all, the Palace has remained, representing stability, identity, and creativity of spirit. Just as the Palace adapted to changing circumstances and needs, so have New Mexico's people adapted for survival.

Artifacts are the physical expression of people's actions and thoughts. As New Mexico's biggest and most important artifact, the Palace symbolizes our common heritage, both violent and peaceful. Its diverse collections, whether regal or commonplace, represent New Mexico's collective values and memory.

In its newest role as a key part of the new history museum, opening in 2009, the Palace will offer the opportunity to look back over the last four hundred years while looking ahead to the next one hundred. History is not a closed

book. Future archaeological techniques and newly found historical documents will allow ongoing interpretation and discoveries about the past. Which Palace policies worked well or poorly? How might reconsidering the Palace's historical role improve our future community?

Because lack of communication and representation has caused so much human misery, historical museums must invite respectful exchange. Thoughtful exhibits and interpretation help us understand our own and other cultures, help heal injustices, and build positive connections to guide our future. Without such knowledge of the past, however, we cannot make these connections.

Together with the new state history museum, a refurbished Palace promises to help visitors appreciate New Mexico's complex past and create a more humanistic next century. Just as it has for the past four hundred years, the Palace will continue to guide public thinking and values. In addition, the Palace will represent New Mexico, highlighting its unique contributions to shaping the nation's identity.

Over the past four centuries, the Palace has served New Mexicans as a capitol, military stronghold, royal residence, prison, market and transportation center, post office, bank, historical society, and museum. The Palace's next century has yet to be written. Will the old adobe survive to celebrate its five hundredth year, enduring as a valuable symbol of past accomplishments? Will our great-grandchildren learn about their culture through Palace events and exhibits? Will the Palace and plaza remain international and intercultural centers for art, education, and commerce?

Only time will tell, but this much is certain: As long as the Palace stands, it will continue to serve, safeguarding the past and preserving the values of New Mexico's diverse population for decades to come.

Bell Ranch chuckwagon, made in 1935 and used until 1961. Photographed in the Palace courtyard. Courtedy Palace of the Governors (DCA/MNM).

References

Adams, Eleanor

1944   Two Colonial New Mexico Libraries: 1704 and 1776. *New Mexico Historical Review* 19(2).

1954   *Bishop Tamaron's Visitation of New Mexico, 1760*. Albuquerque: Historical Society of New Mexico.

Chauvenet, Beatrice

1983   *Hewett and Friends: A Biography of Santa Fe's Vibrant Era*. Santa Fe: Museum of New Mexico Press.

Chávez, Fray Angélico

1949   De Vargas' Negro Drummer. *New Mexico Historical Review* 56(5).

1954   *Origins of New Mexico Families in the Spanish Colonial Period*. Santa Fe: Historical Society of New Mexico.

Chavez, Thomas

1980–81   But Were They All Natives? *El Palacio* 86(4).

1997–98   La Historia de la Nueva México: The Cuartocentenario of Juan de Onate. *El Palacio* 102(2).

Cook, Mary Jean

1993   "Daughters of the Camino Real," in *El Camino Real de Tierra Adentro*, compiled by Gabrielle Palmer, 147-68. Santa Fe: New Mexico Bureau of Land Management.

Hyslop, Stephen

2002   *Bound for Santa Fe.* Norman: University of Oklahoma Press.

Kenner, Charles

1969   *A History of New Mexican–Plains Indian Relations.* Norman: University of Oklahoma Press.

Kessell, John

1980   *The Missions of New Mexico since 1776.* Albuquerque: University of New Mexico Press.

1989   "By Force of Arms: Vargas and the Restoration of Santa Fe," in *Santa Fe: History of an Ancient City,* edited by David Noble, 53–63. Santa Fe: SAR Press.

1989   "Spaniards and Pueblos: From Crusading Intolerance to Pragmatic Accommodation." In *Columbian Consequences,* vol 1, David Hurst Thomas, ed., 127–38. Washington, DC: Smithsonian Institute.

1993   "The Presence of the Past: Pecos Pueblo," in *Pecos Ruins,* edited by David G. Noble, 12–14. Santa Fe: Ancient City Press.

2002   *Spain in the Southwest: A Narrative History of Colonial New Mexico, Arizona, Texas, and California.* Norman: University of Oklahoma Press.

2004   Juan Bautista de Anza, Father and Son. *New Mexico Historical Review* 79(2).

2004   Not That Remote: Diego de Vargas and His Household in Santa Fe. *El Palacio* 109(2–3).

Lecompte, Janet

1985   *Rebellion in Rio Arriba, 1837.* Albuquerque: University of New Mexico Press.

Meadows, Karen

1984   Celebrating the Museum's 75th Year. *El Palacio* 90(2).

Padilla, Jean

1992   "The Santa Fe Concert Band," www.santafeconcertband.org.

Shishkin, J. K.

N.d.   The Unquiet Centuries: A Biography of the Palace of the Governors. Museum of New Mexico Palace of the Governors, Fray Angélico Chávez History Library.

1968   *An Early History of the Museum of New Mexico Fine Arts Building.* Santa Fe: Museum of New Mexico Press.

1972   *The Palace of the Governors.* Albuquerque: Museum of New Mexico, University Printing Plant.

Weber, David

1973   An Unforgettable Day: Facundo Melgares on Independence. *New Mexico Historical Review* 48(1).

Weigle, Marta, and Peter White

1988   *The Lore of New Mexico.* Albuquerque: University of New Mexico Press.